Master Artisans

of the Grands Ateliers de France

Master Artisans

of the Grands Ateliers de France

Jean Bergeron & Catherine Laulhère

Introduction by Laurence Bonnet • Photographs by Jacques Boulay

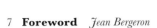

Foreword

I cannot believe that two decades have passed since the Grands Ateliers de France were founded. How time flies. Back then, I could never have imagined having the pleasure and honour of writing this text, even though the life of this community of artisans is also an affair of the heart. I have loved it all these years, and I still love it, because it is built on the finest qualities of the finest people, as personified by its succession of presidents – all very different personalities, but each one just as richly talented as the others. Judge for yourselves:

Michel Germond: disciplined, ethical, with the strictest standards and unfailing loyalty. His experience was essential at the birth of a fine and honourable association that always seeks to achieve the perfect balance between preservation and intervention. This applies as much to the recruitment of its members as to communications with the outside world.

Rémy Brazet: a dynamic, generous, intelligent spirit, with a subtle ability to handle people and to fly our flag with all the necessary vigour and diplomacy – particularly the latter, at a time when diplomacy was badly needed!

Philippe Prutner: his stature was such that he created an atmosphere of calm dedication. His disciplined and prudent management was just what we needed after so many upheavals.

Reinhard von Nagel: ambitious and passionate – a man with integrity and panache who takes pride in his work and finds the right word at the right time; and who left his own culture to embrace and enhance that of France.

Gérard Desquand: a skilled politician who was able to guide the Grands Ateliers through the labyrinths of the professional world and hone the rough edges in order to raise it to the level of a hallowed institution.

Finally, Lison de Caunes: always positive, always enthusiastic, the personification of creativity, whose charm and discreet authority will bring a thoroughly modern femininity to the ongoing history of the Grands Ateliers.

To relive all those years, I went back over the various writings on the Grands Ateliers, and found these words, which I wrote for an exhibition at the Château de Pregny, Switzerland, in 2001: 'We admire, we dream, we fall silent.' It is as true now as it was then.

Jean Bergeron
Founding President

Michel Germond

Furniture restorer
Former President of the Grands Ateliers de France

The Grands Ateliers de France owe a special debt of gratitude to Michel Germond, founder member and President between 1994 and 1997. He played a key role in shaping the association from its modest beginnings to what it is today, but has also made a lasting impact in the fields of cabinetmaking and restoration of 17th- and 18th-century furniture. Although now retired, his legacy – the culmination of fifty years' accumulated knowledge and expertise – lives on.

Throughout his career, Michel has been admired for his efficiency and uncompromising integrity. From 1981, he served the Paris Court of Appeal and still works there in an honorary capacity. He has been in high demand from the great auction houses, notably Christie's, who have been consulting him for almost two decades. Over the years, he also built up a prestigious international clientele that remained with him until his workshop, Atelier Michel Germond, closed in 2011. Today, private clients and public institutions continue to call on his expertise.

Michel has always placed great importance on passing on his skills and has never stinted in sharing his unique experience with younger generations. He puts emphasis on having respect for the original work and its creator, as well as for the client who has entrusted him with the object. He has also devised a new method of restoration, which was initially patented but has now been adopted by some of the major workshops. Clients hold him in great esteem – a point that was highlighted when he was given a unique paperweight in Boulle marquetry that he had formerly restored, a unique gift in homage to a man who knew how to appreciate and preserve its beauty better than anyone else.

Twenty Years of the Grands Ateliers de France

This book celebrates the twentieth anniversary of the Grands Ateliers. In its way, it is a bridge across time, since the founding of the association was also marked by the publication of a book, entitled *Mains et Merveilles* (1993), which featured 360 of the best artisans in Paris.

One of those artisans, Marie Brocard, a restorer of embroideries and tapestries, was visited at her Paris workshop by Jean Bergeron, former president of the Comité Colbert, a prestigious association of luxury brands. She asked whether he would consider setting up a similar society for artisans. He replied: 'Find me artisans who deserve one.' A week later, she had convinced everyone working with her on the restoration of the Empress's bedchamber at the Château de Fontainebleau that this was a good idea.

Thus it was that the first meeting of the Grands Ateliers took place. Crafts represented included the embroidery of Marie Brocard, the wall hangings of the Maison Brazet, the bronzes of the Maison Meilleur, the cabinetmaking of the Atelier Michel Germond, and the gilding of the Maison Alot. A strict code of selection was agreed upon, based on the ethics of each artisan, the quality of his or her work, a respect for both object and client, and a requirement that all restoration work should be reversible, to prevent any temptation to deceive. New members had to be nominated by two existing members, and a secret ballot would be held every year at the Annual General Meeting, with a 60 per cent majority required for election. Presidents would be chosen by the Council of Administration, for a non-renewable three-year term of office.

And so the Grands Ateliers were founded, with Jean Bergeron as their first president; Laurence Bonnet, journalist and author of *Mains et Merveilles*, was appointed executive officer, and the founding members were the five well-respected workshops named above. There was also an honorary committee presided over by the Nobel prizewinner Pierre-Gilles de Gennes, with Hélène David-Weill and Catherine Deneuve as vice-presidents.

Despite some departures due to retirement and other factors, the number of members has now increased fifteenfold. Almost a hundred disciplines are represented, with some artisans specializing in different fields of conservation and restoration, while others produce original work. Friendships and collaborations between members have grown, and the scope of the association has expanded well beyond what was initially envisaged.

Throughout this period, the Grands Ateliers have publicized their work through an impressive series of exhibitions. Here are some of the highlights.

January 1995: *Les Ors du Temps*, Le Marais, Paris

Inside a small private house that was about to be renovated, the twenty-eight members of the Grands Ateliers held an exhibition of their treasures amid the rubble, over the space of a long weekend. A long band of linen guided the visitors, who were given pocket torches to help them focus on the fine details of each work. Designed to attract the media and gain wider recognition from potential clients and the public, the exhibition welcomed 8,000 visitors in four days, despite recent floods in Paris, with a queue stretching all along the Rue du Foin. Entry was free and all 2,000 catalogues were sold.

October–November 1996: *Mains et Merveilles*, Couvent des Cordeliers, Paris

'Paris celebrates its arts and crafts' was the exhibition subtitle, and its aim was to bring the work of the Grands Ateliers to the attention of a wider audience. The overarching concept was based on the fact that the raw materials used by the artisans originated from different countries and the finished works often ended up being shipped to international destinations, but the expertise used to shape them came from France. Throughout the 1,000 square metres (10,750 sq. ft) of exhibition space, crates filled with wood fibre were used to display glittering gilded objects; wooden pallets were piled up into platforms to show off striking pieces; a huge curtain of saffron yellow silk was hung from a folding ladder. There were also workshops for children, with paper, fabrics and other materials supplied by the artisans; lectures on the arts and crafts; evening harpsichord recitals, and a commemorative medal designed by Jean-Luc Seigneur and struck by the visitors themselves. Results far exceeded expectations: thirty-five ateliers, free entry, and nearly 100,000 visitors over twenty days, thanks largely to extensive press and TV coverage.

1998: Two shows in Chicago

Following invitations from French consul Gérard Dumont, as part of the 'Fête de France' festival, and from Chris Kennedy, owner of Chicago's Merchandise Mart, the Atelier held two exhibitions, one at the Decorex USA trade fair, and one at the Neiman Marcus department store. Some twenty-seven workshops were represented, including artisans who spoke no English or had never flown before. The Decorex award for best speaker went to the future executive officer of the Grands Ateliers, Stefan Geissler.

September 2001: *Objets Précieux, Objets Curieux, Matériaux Rares et Métiers Rares*, Château de Pregny, near Geneva

An exhibition that brought together the finest creations and restored pieces by forty-three members of the Grands Ateliers, using materials such as ivory, tortoiseshell and exotic woods. This private exhibition was generously sponsored by the Maurice and Noémie de Rothschild Foundation for Art, through Benjamin and Ariane de Rothschild, and was scheduled for the weekend of 13 September 2001. Attendance was badly affected by the repercussions of the events of 11 September in New York, but the show was much admired by those who were able to see it.

October 2002: Hôtel de Wendel, Paris

In anticipation of their tenth anniversary, the Grands Ateliers were welcomed by art collector Franz Wassmer for a one-night mini-exhibition.

June 2003: *Objets d'Orgueil*, Couvent des Cordeliers, Paris

Designed as a sparkling celebration of the Grands Ateliers' tenth anniversary, with forty-two workshops representing forty-three crafts. Elegantly staged, each display tailored to fit the work, and a grand opening with nearly 4,000 guests. However, a strike by media workers, including TV cameramen, meant that coverage of the exhibition was lower than expected. Under the title *Objets de Passion: Les Grands Ateliers*, Elise de Moncan produced a striking book of photographs taken at the exhibition.

Friends of the Grands Ateliers

SAGA (Société des Amis des Grands Ateliers) was founded in September 2007 after a campaign by faithful clients, under the honorary presidency of Pierre-Christian Taittinger, who was also head of the Délégation du Commerce, de l'Artisanat, des Professions Libérales et des Métiers d'Art. The aim of SAGA is to promote awareness of French arts and crafts.

The Grands Ateliers become the Grands Ateliers de France

The Grands Ateliers were invited by the Syndicat des Antiquaires to demonstrate their expertise, precision and attention to detail in the collectors' salon beneath the glass roof of the Grand Palais, Paris. The show then toured France and the rest of Europe.

2008: *Artigianato e Palazzo*, Giardino Corsini, Florence

2008: *Winter Fine Arts and Antiques Fair*, Olympia, London

2009: *Dans l'Intimité des Grands Ateliers*, Paris

Exhibition held at the Ateliers de Paris in the Faubourg Saint-Antoine.

2009–10: *100% Fait Main*, Villa Demoiselle, Reims

Exhibition in the cellars of a beautiful Art Nouveau/Art Deco villa, sponsored by Paul-François and Nathalie Vranken, owners of the Pommery and Demoiselle champagne house. This was followed by another exhibition at the same location: *Or en Désordre*.

2010: *Couleurs d'Ateliers*, Palais Royal, Paris

This large-scale window display at the Palais Royal was organized in collaboration with the French Ministry of Culture, as part of the exhibition series *Métiers d'Art en Scène*.

September 2010: *Hors les Murs à Monaco*

A four-day exhibition at the Port Palace, Monte Carlo.

October 2011 and 2012: *Rencontres de Pommard*, Château de Pommard, Burgundy

Exhibitions held at the invitation of the château's owner, Maurice Giraud.

September 2013: *Le Temps Traversé*, Grand Palais, Paris

As part of 'Revelations, Paris 21st century', in the premier salon for crafts and the creative arts, a highly prestigious exhibition in celebration of the Grands Ateliers' twentieth anniversary.

For an association of this kind to have not only lasted for twenty years but to have grown and thrived in this way is a rare and extraordinary thing. To mark this, the Grands Ateliers website has been redesigned and relaunched to maximize its flexibility, simplicity and speed. The site was first launched in 1996, with the support of American patron George Parker Jr. and French government minister Jean-Pierre Raffarin.

Laurence Bonnet

Pierre Bonnefille
ATELIER PIERRE BONNEFILLE
Painter and furniture designer

Christian Broggini
LA MAISON LUMIÈRE
Lighting architect

Lison de Caunes
Straw marquetry artist

Marine Fouquet & Hervé Morin
ATELIER MAONIA
Furniture designers and marquetry artists

Mireille Herbst
ALM DÉCO
Lacquer artist

Xavier, Johann & Bruno Lemerle
LEMERLE FRÈRES
Upholsterers

Marie Le Cœur
Fabric painter

Anne Nicolle
Ornamental woodcarver

Mehdi Mallier
DUNOD-MALLIER
Wrought-iron worker and metalworker

Bernard Pictet
Glassworker

Steaven Richard
ATELIER STEAVEN RICHARD
Artisan metalworker

CHAPTER 1

Interior Beauty

Pierre Bonnefille

ATELIER PIERRE BONNEFILLE

Painter and furniture designer

Richard Strauss's *Capriccio* (1942) reflects on an issue that has long preoccupied opera: which is more important, the words or the music? Pierre Bonnefille's unique polychromatic wall murals and pieces of furniture might prompt a similar question: does the colour take precedence over the material, or vice versa? However, this talented manipulator of medium bypasses the question and simply does his own thing.

Pierre has benefited from the support of master cabinetmaker Michel Germond, the embodiment of classical excellence (see page 9). We need only look at Pierre's furniture to understand why. The murals offer something different: they arouse our curiosity and are full of surprises, with a vocabulary that varies according to their setting.

Pierre draws from the great well of nature – from the landscape, the forest, the desert, the seashore – where earth and leaves, sand and shells, form a palette of materials and colours that are never fixed but constantly evolving. The leaves on a tree change colour with the seasons and eventually break down into humus. Pierre's hand narrates this story of life and death, of matter decomposing, in a form of metaphysics that he would never label as such but simply expresses through his work. Sometimes Pierre does choose words, but like organic material they are difficult to grasp, and transform themselves according to a particular time or context. What he writes is nothing but the volatility of language, which he fixes on a canvas, a mural or an item of furniture.

There is something Florentine about Pierre Bonnefille: he has a similar talent to those artists whose patrons allowed them to give full rein to their art. His clients – private individuals, designers, companies, institutions – have had the good sense not to place any restrictions on his creative flair. Each work establishes itself with a few strokes of the pencil; his pigments come from all over the world to create a contemporary alchemy whose promise is already apparent from the very first sketch. And his promise is always kept, if not surpassed. Bearing witness to this is a monumental work composed of dark blues to harmonize with the London night skies, and installed at the top of Renzo Piano's Shard.

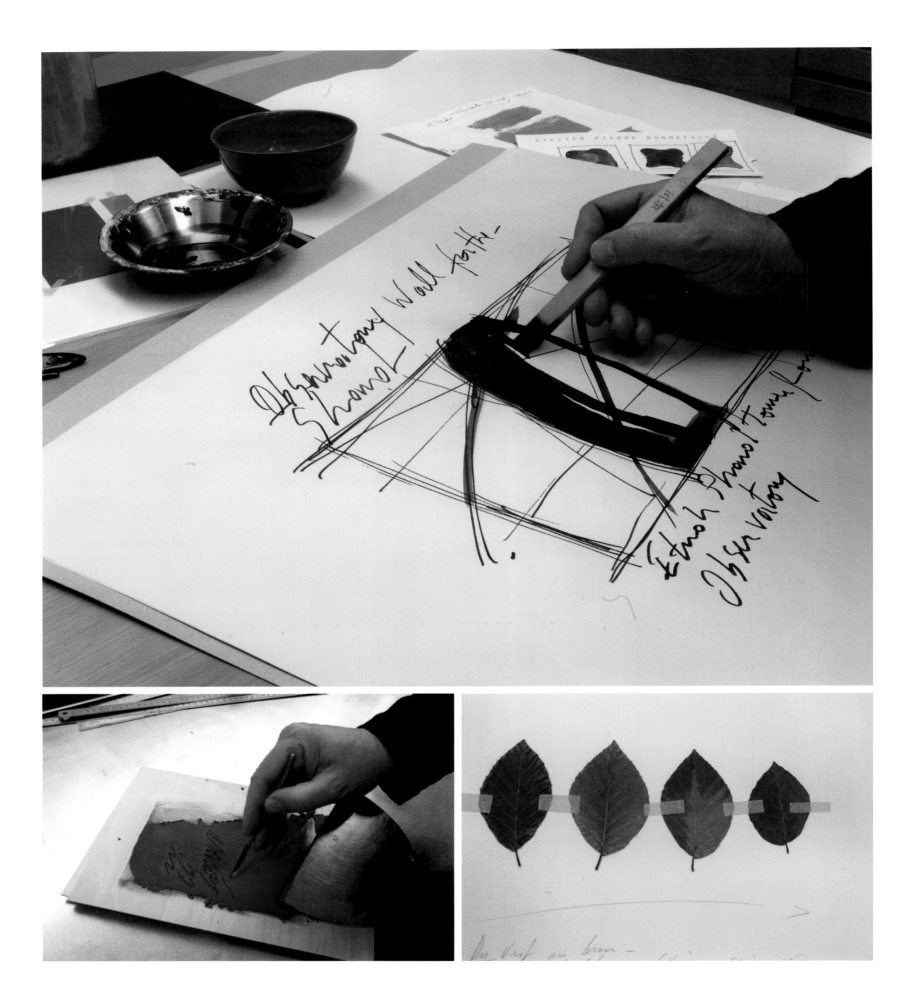

Christian Broggini

LA MAISON LUMIÈRE

Lighting architect

Christian Broggini's first love is the theatre – a space that is typically in use day and night – where light, of course, plays a starring role. Light can show objects off to their best advantage, picking out details and drawing our attention to them, throwing them into relief, emphasizing their elegance, their associations, their warmth, their solidity, their transparency. 'The theatre is the most beautiful place in the world!' exclaims Christian, who spent years displaying his lighting talents on stage before letting them loose on the world of haute couture. He has provided lighting for the shows and shops of some of the most prestigious fashion houses, including Jean Paul Gaultier, Christian Lacroix, Yves Saint Laurent and Christian Dior.

Christian has also lent his talents to less flamboyant projects. He works for private clients, often collectors, alongside interior designers such as Agnès Comar and Jacques Grange, and admires the originality shown by this younger generation of creatives. He believes lighting should be taken into account right from the start of any project, together with the architect's plans, but this is not always the case. La Maison Lumière, which is a family business, makes sure it is on location as early as possible to bring light to the new space.

For Christian, one of the joys of his craft lies in meeting people, because the choice of lighting must always reflect the character of the person living with it. A great deal of discussion takes place with the client to ensure that the lighting falls on the right objects. This task is made much easier by the innovation of LED lighting, which can be both powerful and precisely focused, highlighting individual items in a collection, articles of furniture, and particular areas within a space. It can also be used for difficult projects such as the Bordeauxthèque in the Galeries Lafayette, where the lights must not influence the temperature by more than half a degree so as not to affect the conservation and natural ageing of the finest wines on display. Christian spends a lot of time working with museums, where there is now an increasing awareness that exhibited works require not only targeted display but also protection from light damage. His clients include the Musée des Beaux-Arts in Rennes and the Manufacture des Gobelins in Paris.

Lison de Caunes

Straw marquetry artist

Lison de Caunes may well have dreamt her first dreams in a cradle of straw, or perhaps shagreen. Surrounded by her grandfather's works from the moment she was born, she explored a natural gift that had simply skipped a generation. Her family is a microcosm of 20th-century artistic talents. Paul Poiret and Jeanne Boivin belonged to the same generation as her grandmother and grandfather, the famous designer André Groult. Lison has inherited her mother's free spirit and knows exactly what she wants – to keep working with her hands as long as she possibly can. She began with bookbinding and went on to learn cabinetmaking, all the while surrounded by her grandfather's pieces, his tools and his straw. Only his workshop had disappeared. At first she applied his materials to books without realizing that this was simply the prelude to an adventure on a greater scale.

During the second half of the 1970s, Art Deco experienced a revival and, in the windows of the antique shops on the Rue du Bac in Paris, Lison discovered items of furniture signed by the interior designer Jean-Michel Frank. She unearthed shagreens in the flea market, and some 19th-century straw marquetry caskets also caught her eye. All these objects had aged very badly and were in urgent need of attention. Her grandfather's famous folding screen, even after cleaning, had also lost its former lustre. Straw catches and radiates light when it has been properly worked. Lison is passionate about this humble, seemingly fragile material that can be transformed into something genuinely luxurious. She taught herself how to work with straw and thus launched herself into a new career.

In 1992, the Forney Library in Paris mounted an exhibition at which Lison displayed 200 objects of straw marquetry. Her grandfather's work recovered its lost lustre, and with all the necessary precision and attention to detail, Lison restored, repaired, cut and smoothed the sheaves of straw that he had left her. A chair rusher in Fontainebleau and a cereal farmer in Burgundy were to be her future suppliers. She does the dyeing in her kitchen, and the shaping and gluing in the workshop, spending countless hours giving new life to the tiniest objects or to large surfaces designed to cover a wall or to be applied to a wooden item. She stretches this material to the very limits of its capacity, and so the humble straw of the stable becomes fit for the finest of palaces.

Lison also works closely with a cabinetmaker, and creates contemporary decorative objects that are popular with such luxury brands as Louis Vuitton and famous American designers such as Peter Marino. In 1998, Lison was given the title of *maître d'art*, which set an official seal on the creative work in which she takes such pride. She loves her artistic freedom, is most at home in her workshop, and for the last twenty years has taken on apprentices in order to pass on her knowledge and perhaps also, just occasionally, to feel less isolated.

Marine Fouquet
& Hervé Morin

ATELIER MAONIA
Furniture designers and marquetry artists

Marine Fouquet studied at the École des Beaux-Arts in Paris, specializing in furniture, and has been awarded the title of Meilleur Ouvrier de France, a prestigious distinction that honours the very best French craftsmen and craftswomen. Meanwhile, Hervé Morin studied cabinetmaking at the École Boulle. Shortly after they had been invited to join the Grands Ateliers de France, they began to work together for interior designers, merging their complementary skills.

Both are continually on the lookout for new combinations of materials, although Hervé is particularly gifted in using different media to achieve creative effects, from ebony to parchment. Mother-of-pearl, bone, shagreen and stainless steel are all used, and Hervé searches the world over for rare woods, sometimes buying them on the internet, but also travelling to the forests to see the wood for himself. 'We learn a lot from our suppliers,' he says. Marine's strength, on the other hand, lies in her imagination and design skill, and she finds particular pleasure in straw marquetry.

Marine and Hervé like to experiment with form as well as with materials. Lamps, bedheads for ships, high heels for Roger Vivier – there is no limit to the variety of their work or their talents, which range from cabinetmaking to carving, from art to design. Jacques Grange, Louis Vuitton, Fendi and Chanel are on their list of clients, which continues to grow. The Atelier Maonia, which is named after a shrub, is on an endless quest for creative originality, aiming to change our perception of the materials used.

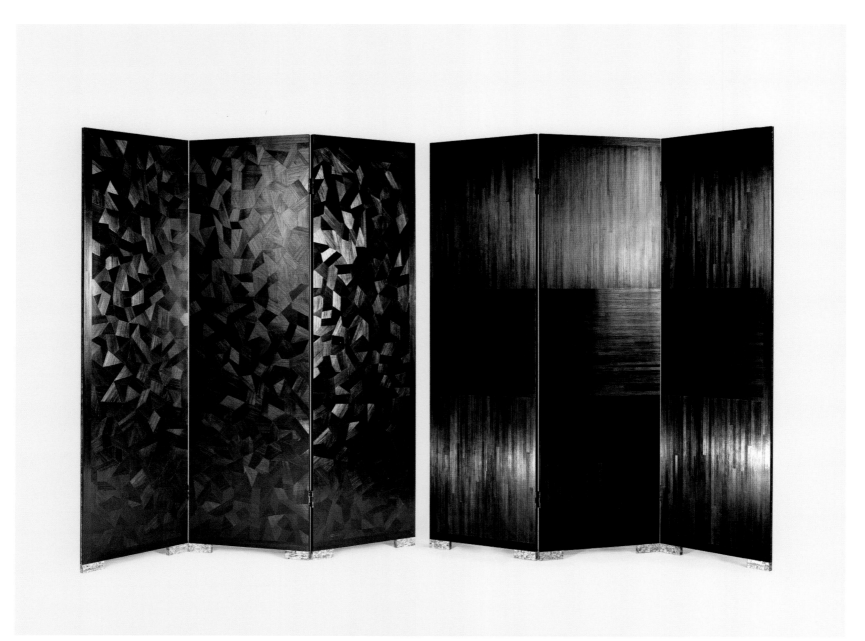

Mireille Herbst

ALM DÉCO
Lacquer artist

Mireille Herbst found her calling as a lacquer artist purely by chance. In 1974, having studied graphic arts at the Lycée Auguste Renoir in Paris, she answered a small advertisement from a lacquer artist seeking someone with drawing skills. In her search for a job, the young Mireille had found a career, and lacquer has been her passion ever since.

Preparation of the object is critical before the many layers of lacquer are applied, so as to prevent any marks or imperfections on the surface from showing up. This is a lesson that Mireille seems to have taken on board in her professional career also, patiently learning all the techniques of the craft through practice.

Having gained experience in three different workshops, she then moved to the most prestigious atelier of the time, Saïn et Tambuté. In 1994, she founded ALM Déco, which took over the Saïn et Tambuté workshops. Today, her clients are mainly designers and other creative workers.

Xavier, Johann & Bruno Lemerle

LEMERLE FRÈRES
Upholsterers

It was Xavier and Bruno's father, Marcel, who set up this workshop in the 17th arrondissement of Paris in 1957. Marcel never asked his sons to work with him, although he expected them to, and it was Bruno, the youngest, who first joined him at the age of twenty-two, after training as a cabinet-maker – 'because I loved working with my hands!' he says. Xavier, on the other hand, began his adult life as an electrophysicist but soon tired of it and moved around a lot before finally settling down in the family workshop. Xavier's son Johann studied leathercraft and upholstery, served apprenticeships with Hermès and Louis Vuitton, and then joined his father and uncle.

In terms of skill, the Lemerles are equally matched, alternating between hand-dyeing leather with natural pigments (their speciality), upholstering chairs and other items of furniture, and applying patina to parchment and animal skins. They work for museums and collectors, restoring furniture from the 17th and 18th centuries – a task that often involves the reapplication of sheet metal such as gold leaf and the use of original tools. The Lemerle family also has a pattern book that helps them to identify precisely what is required for each commission. Nowadays, their services are much in demand from interior designers, and they receive commissions from all over the world, with clients such as Peter Marino and Frank de Biasi turning to them to select and dye the finest skins.

Xavier, Bruno and Johann all demonstrate the same close attention to detail and willingness to start from scratch until they have achieved perfection. However, although they continually exchange views about the various options and estimates, it is Xavier who is in charge of administration.

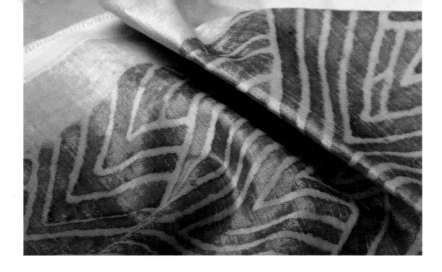

Marie Le Cœur

Fabric painter

Marie Le Cœur studied painting at the École Nationale Supérieure des Arts Décoratifs in Paris, but it was on entering the theatre that she decided to become a fabric painter and started to acquire the technical expertise necessary for her profession. She draws inspiration from motifs of the past, although she rarely engages in restoration, applying her designs in paint to new, durable fabrics. She is equally adept at creating decors for the interiors of apartments (painted winter gardens, ceilings or blinds, for example).

Among her many attributes is a close attention to detail. In her profession, even the slightest mistake can have disastrous consequences and ultimately ruin the piece. Preparation must therefore be as thorough as possible, both in terms of the maquettes that she creates before starting on a project and her stencils, which are sometimes cut under a magnifying glass. The paints are also prepared in advance and measured to a tenth of a millilitre. No matter what she is working on, Marie must always combine precision and technical mastery with the poetic, aesthetic side of the creation, bringing out the details that allow the colours to take their full effect.

Marie works mainly with interior designers and theatre specialists, who often introduce her to new clients from other countries. Her extraordinary talent for recapturing the styles of past centuries using modern techniques has won her great admiration. In order to give her fabrics the appearance of age, she often undertakes extensive research. For instance, she makes up the colours that were used centuries ago, which requires a highly trained eye and a rare sense of measurement. Researching motifs of the past can also be a time-consuming process.

She approaches her work in a similar way to a restorer, or indeed a forger, spending hours trying to fathom the aspirations and technical particularities of her predecessors. Painting fabrics also means understanding the texture of the material and how paint reacts to various media: it behaves differently when applied to silk than it does on wool or velvet. Knowing all these things inside out is what makes Marie such a rare talent.

Anne Nicolle

Ornamental woodcarver

Anne Nicolle was inspired by nature and, in particular, her love of trees and horses. On finishing her baccalaureate, she began to look for a career that united these two passions. From an early age, her parents encouraged her to develop her talent for drawing, and woodcarving seemed a natural step. The eminent sculptor Jean Renouvel taught her the craft of carving wood.

For Anne, ornamentation is to woodcarving what music theory is to musical interpretation. Ornamental woodcarving demands discipline and precision, as well as an insatiable cultural curiosity. There is very little latitude in this sphere, and the professional and artistic requirements are stringent.

While she has continued to restore pieces for antique dealers and private clients, over the past few years she has increasingly focused on her creative side, producing elegant animal carvings. Passing on her own knowledge is also an integral part of Anne's life, and for many years she has offered evening courses in ornamental carving at the École Boulle.

Located at the heart of the prestigious Marais quarter in Paris, Anne's workshop is an inexhaustible source of enchantment. Bathed in light, her workbench is covered with an array of gouges, mallets and chisels, and all around are her wonderful woodcarvings, each bearing witness to her mastery of this traditional decorative art.

Mehdi Mallier

DUNOD-MALLIER
Wrought-iron worker and metalworker

Ironwork is a vast subject area, encompassing pieces from the period of Louis XIII through to Edgar Brandt and the present day. This diversity also characterizes Mehdi Mallier's approach to his craft, which brings him closer to literature, descriptive geometry and even poetry. He sees artisan metalwork as a springboard to the fine arts themselves.

The combination of metal and art fascinated Mehdi from an early age. He was sixteen when he came upon a monumental sculpture, *Le Taureau (The Bull)* by Serge Marchal, an artist who shares his passion for metal. Mehdi began an apprenticeship with the Compagnons du Tour de France, a French organization of craftsmen and artisans, but it was the culture of the forge that attracted him – working with fire and with a material so difficult to master but so rewarding to mould. He visited and worked in ateliers all over the world, rediscovering his childhood pleasure of drawing.

Design is approached in a modern way, sometimes using computers, but the techniques of fabrication remain traditional, as do the tools. Measurements are taken, the object is made in the workshop, and finally the piece is installed in its rightful place. This is the daily routine of the wrought-iron worker, and every item he makes is a prototype. Mehdi moulds all kinds of metal, including iron, copper, brass and stainless steel, and works with blocks; he then assembles the pieces in the old-fashioned way, preferring to use hundreds of screws rather than soldering. There must be absolute trust between the artisan and his clients, and Mehdi is proud of the professional relationships he has formed. He sees every project through to completion and guarantees the highest possible standards, even if this means countless hours of overtime.

Although his own workshop is very much characterized by the 'French touch', Mehdi admires the American forges of the 1930s that constructed the doors of the great Manhattan banks. Commissions of this nature are in decline these days: most of the orders are for stairways and banisters, doors and windows in stainless steel or brass, and the occasional item of furniture. One piece in which the workshop takes special pride is a banister inspired by the grand staircase at the Château de Chantilly.

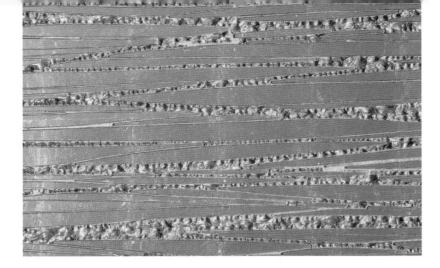

Bernard Pictet

Glassworker

For more than thirty years, Bernard Pictet has been embellishing glass with original, timeless decorations, and his long association with architects, interior designers and plastic artists has opened up a wide range of aesthetic fields. His exceptional talents have earned him commissions from all over the world, often on the recommendation of famous designers, and around 80 per cent of his work is exported. His work adorns the communal spaces of company headquarters, luxury goods manufacturers, hotels and museums, as well as homes and yachts.

Bernard only works to order and is continually creating new designs, usually in close collaboration with his clients. For him, each product is the result of a creative partnership between the architect who provides the space, the environment that dictates the nature of the object, and the workshop that makes the materials, provides the technical expertise, and finally gives reality to the original idea. He also works with artists, transforming their visions into glass.

The workshop draws inspiration from every period of the decorative arts during the design stage and offers its clients a wide variety of options before producing their bespoke item. Bernard and his team are masters of many techniques, including sandblasting and other forms of engraving, and coldworking, as well as offering a variety of finishes.

The team are also interested in kinetic art, a form of art that depends on movement for its effect, creating glass objects whose appearance alters as the observer moves around, and in optics, which can provide surprising decorative effects. They also work with video artists using back projection and reflection, and are exploring the potential of architectural glass. This innovative and versatile approach to Bernard's craft, both technical and artistic, is what makes his workshop so individual and perfectly suited to creating exclusive objects.

Steaven Richard

ATELIER STEAVEN RICHARD

Artisan metalworker

Steaven Richard has never been associated with any company, but for many years preferred to combine travel with learning his craft. For ten years he went from one workshop to another across Germany, England, Ireland and France. He went to the Ateliers Beaux-Arts Centre Glacière in Paris to complete his classical training, but found it came naturally to him to express his creativity in a contemporary manner. Today, he continues to reinterpret traditional works in a modern style: his library ladders are made of titanium, his lamps of steel, his floors of nickel.

Steaven settled in Paris, returning to an area of small workshops with which he had been familiar as a child during the 1980s. In the historic 11th arrondissement he was lucky enough to find a workshop complete with a forge dating back more than 150 years. Despite all the changes that this district has gone through, Steaven's workshop is a little oasis that has preserved all the smells, colours and sounds of metallurgy through the ages. He and his team work for private clients, interior designers, large companies, and institutions such as the Mémorial de la Shoah and the Musée du Quai Branly. Thanks to his professional experience and his creative imagination, he is always able to extract the full artistic potential from the metals he works with, while fulfilling the requirements of his clients.

In 2012, Steaven Richard's workshop produced a floor of 100 square metres (1,075 sq. ft) for the luxurious offices of Shirine Zirak and Karl Lagerfeld. It consists of three layers: a metal base, a layer of plywood and, on top, a layer of nickel. This alloy structure was made with hammer and chisel to create an extraordinarily fine texture. The rivets were also specially made, and the whole project was carried out using traditional techniques and time-honoured skills.

Patrick Blanchard
ATELIER PATRICK BLANCHARD
Woodcarver and restorer

Alain Bouchardon
ATELIER ALAIN BOUCHARDON
Restorer of oil paintings and relining specialist

Rémy Brazet
MAISON BRAZET
Upholsterer of chairs, curtains and wall hangings

Caroline Corrigan
Restorer of works of art on paper

Youri Dmitrenko
ART & ORS
Restorer of gilded and polychrome wood

Marie Dubost
Gilder and restorer of gilded and painted wood

Simon-Pierre Étienne
ATELIER SIMON-PIERRE ÉTIENNE
Cabinetmaker and restorer of furniture and objets d'art

Sébastien Evain
ATELIER SÉBASTIEN EVAIN
Restorer of 18th-century furniture

Gwénola Le Masson
ATELIER L'AMARANTE
Restorer of painted furniture and other painted objects

Rachida Mallogi
Restorer of antique tapestries

Fernando Moreira
Restorer of 17th- and 18th-century gilded bronze and cabinet work

Aude Vieweger de Cordoüe & Thomas Vieweger
ATELIER ARTIS
Sculpture restorers

CHAPTER 2

Preserving the Past

Patrick Blanchard

ATELIER PATRICK BLANCHARD

Woodcarver and restorer

Patrick Blanchard studied at the École Boulle and has taught there for more than a quarter of a century. His work as a teacher reflects the artisan's desire to perpetuate his craft, save it from oblivion, and preserve the knowledge that goes with it. Precision, attention to detail, a creative spark – these are the qualities on which Patrick draws in his quest to keep it alive.

In his workshop in Enghien-les-Bains, in the northern suburbs of Paris, he is equally devoted to restoration, reconstruction and decoration. His technical mastery has long been recognized – in 1997, he was awarded the title of Meilleur Ouvrier de France for his craft – but he is also a creative artist. He is so proficient in the techniques of woodcarving and restoration that it comes as second nature to him to explore and exploit the materials to their very limits. Applying traditional techniques to contemporary pieces, he breathes new life into his work, sometimes collaborating with other designers.

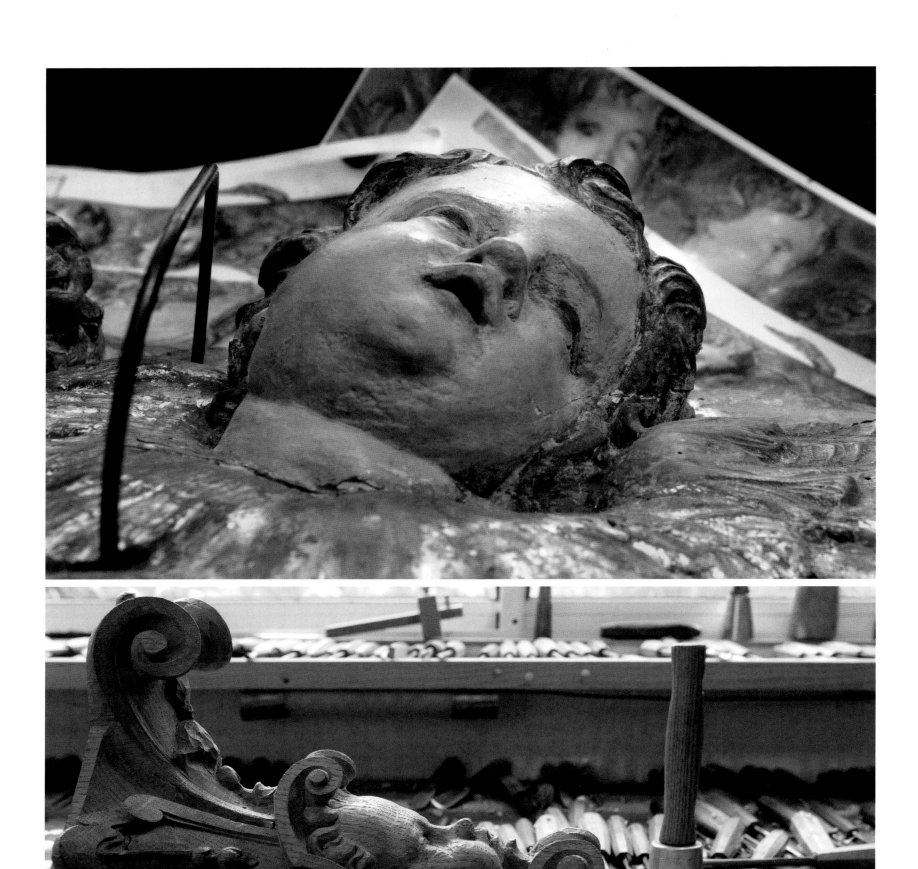

Alain Bouchardon

ATELIER ALAIN BOUCHARDON

Restorer of oil paintings and relining specialist

Alain Bouchardon is the embodiment of the classical traditions that he has loved since he was a student at the École des Beaux-Arts in Paris, where he was taught by Étienne Martin. Then he met Moras, a restorer at the Louvre, and spent several years restoring the paintings of prominent and lesser-known artists. Alain may not have followed in the footsteps of his father, who made watches for Cartier, but he shares the same patience and attention to detail. Such are his skills that he was given the keys to the Palace of Versailles, with the task of restoring a gallery in which the works had suffered considerable damage as a result of vandalism. The restoration work took him twelve years to complete. Since finishing this project, he has been in constant demand from museums and galleries.

A restorer strives to conserve the original painting while remaining faithful to it. Some artworks need cleaning or relining before work can begin on the painting itself. With others, the damage is so severe that the restorer has to 'complete' the picture – for example, if a canvas has torn. The nature of this profession requires a high level of cultural knowledge because restoration means rediscovering the original work – whether it is on canvas, wood, cardboard, paper or copper – even if the materials are not identical to those used by the artist at that time or place.

Alain has lived in Senlis, northern France, since 1976. Among his many accomplishments, he has renovated the ceilings of the renowned jeweler Chaumet in Paris. Sometimes he travels thousands of miles to advise collectors or restore family heirlooms to their former glory. Whether he has been asked to repair a torn painting or the cover of a book, his eye never falters, his hand never wavers, and his judgment remains sound. He is now so experienced that he can tell the age of a canvas by the way it was woven. Describing himself as an archivist, cook, chemist, joiner and artist, he has always been keen to pass on his knowledge to those learning the craft and lends his expertise in a judging capacity to competitions such as the Meilleurs Ouvriers de France.

Depending on the condition of the work, the restorer has two options: starting either with the support material (canvas, wood, copper, etc.) or with the layers of paint. If the work has to be relined, a 'facing' tissue is applied to the surface of the painting to protect it, and the canvas is taken off its stretcher and held at the edges. A new canvas is bonded onto the old from behind, with the aid of a heat-sensitive animal glue that is absorbed by the support. This operation stops any flaking and stabilizes the paint. The restorer can also strengthen the original canvas by fastening it to a solid support, such as a wall or a board – a technique known as *marouflage*.

In more straightforward cases, where relining is not required, the restorer can work directly on the pigment, stabilizing it where necessary, cleaning, smoothing the varnish, touching up any defects, filling in gaps, and adding a final protective layer of varnish. Each work is different and requires fidelity to the materials and techniques employed by the painter (support, preparation, paint, varnish) as well as to the period. The restorer must adapt to all of these constraints and be flexible in his or her approach. In accordance with a universal code of ethics, every restoration must be reversible.

Rémy Brazet

MAISON BRAZET

Upholsterer of chairs, curtains and wall hangings

Neither the bedroom of Marie Antoinette nor the Emperor's Chamber at the Château de Fontainebleau holds any secrets for Rémy Brazet. He knows every detail of the wall hangings, the curtains, the bedheads and the armchairs. The restoration of the Emperor's Chamber was a project that he inherited in 1994, following the sudden death of his father, who founded Atelier Jacques Brazet. Jacques set up the business soon after the Second World War, swiftly gaining recognition as one of the best upholsterers of his generation, and during the 1960s went into partnership with Jean-Dominique Serres, a designer for the couturier Jacques Fath.

Rémy was not always committed to following in his father's footsteps: at sixteen he considered turning his back on the profession but saw the light while studying at the École du Louvre in Paris, where he discovered a passion for examining and working with materials. He joined his father in 1983 and learned all the tricks of the trade, from creating curves to sculpting horsehair. In 1996, he invented and perfected a technique for preserving and restoring ancient wood, and his reputation spread far and wide.

Radiating good humour and warmth, Rémy creates an atmosphere of cheerful efficiency that reflects the rewarding nature of his craft. As a *maître d'art*, he has restored some of the finest pieces in the history of 18th-century furniture, his favourite period. Atelier Jacques Brazet has been in demand from a string of world-renowned French museums, including the Malmaison, Versailles, Musée Galliera, Musée des Arts Décoratifs, Carnavalet, Cognacq-Jay, Dapper and Nissim de Camondo. When the J. Paul Getty Museum in Los Angeles commissioned him to restore its *Lit à la Polonaise*, an 18th-century four-poster bed, the Atelier acquired a faithful American clientele, including the famous Vanderbilt family. Other prestigious American museums followed suit – the Museum of Fine Arts in Boston, the Minneapolis Institute of Arts, and the Marble House in Newport, Rhode Island, among others.

The hunt for materials identical to the originals is never simple, but it is the trademark of the Maison Brazet that every item of furniture is given the respect it deserves. The company works with the finest producers of textiles and soft furnishings to ensure that it uses the correct fabrics and weaves. There can be no substitute for a silk brocatelle or a Genoa velvet, and fidelity to the original would not be possible without a technical mastery and enviable knowledge of the period and piece.

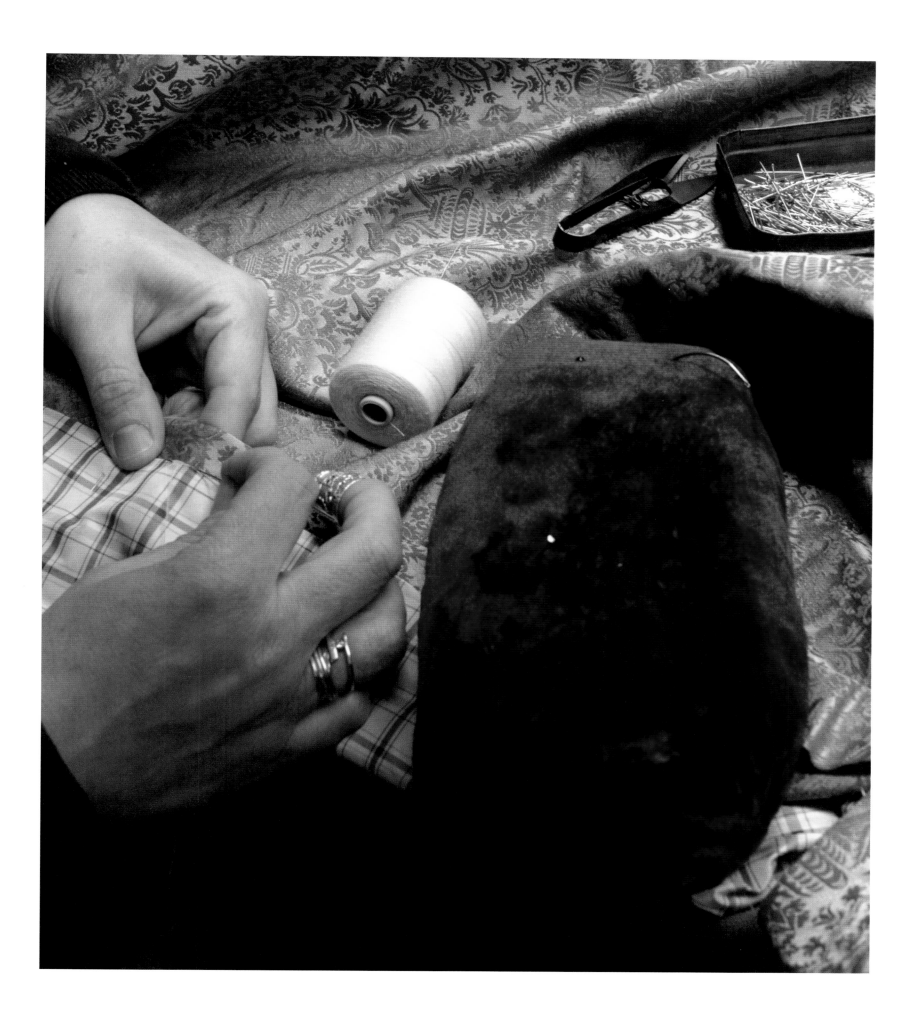

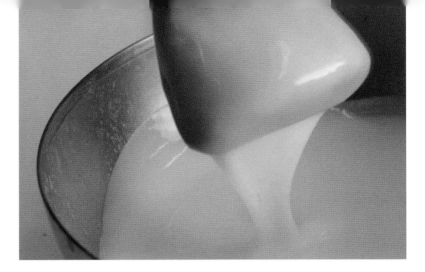

Caroline Corrigan

Restorer of works of art on paper

Caroline Corrigan is extremely patient and meticulous – qualities that you might expect of someone who restores drawings for a living. Working for museums, collectors and art dealers, she cleans, retouches and sometimes restores the colours, focusing on one tiny area of paper at a time with the aid of a magnifying glass and bright light. The media used might be pencil, ink or charcoal. In consultation with the owner of the drawing, she reconstructs the original colour palette and repairs damage from tears, mould and light exposure, although she would never go so far as to recreate a missing section.

Caroline has always loved drawing, but she began her career as a speech therapist. She is an expert listener who takes pride in adapting her restorative skills to her clients' precise requirements. She likes to imagine the history of the drawings, which often have to tell their own story because in most cases they are not signed. Millimetre by millimetre, with obsessive attention to detail, she allows her intuition to guide her – although she insists that outside work, she is the exact opposite.

She starts by removing lining and mounting boards from the back of the drawing, using steam, a large vacuum pump, a scalpel and alcohol. She must remove not only the lining or mount to which the drawing is fixed, but also the glue, which is often of poor quality and can hinder restoration. The next step involves copious use of blotting paper to absorb the alcohol, which makes the paper more porous and therefore more accessible. Another major obstacle to restoration is dust, which over time clings to every particle of the paper.

Caroline's workshop might be compared to a laboratory or an operating theatre, within which she must make her incisions without causing injury to the main body of the work. That is why sometimes the palette knife takes over from the scalpel. Once the drawing has been removed, Japanese paper is applied like a bandage, so that it can be manipulated more easily. Caroline's touch is sure and precise, with a confidence that comes partly from experience, but perhaps also from the fact that she comes from a long line of artists, including many women with distinct talents of their own.

Youri Dmitrenko

ART & ORS
Restorer of gilded and polychrome wood

Youri Dmitrenko decided on his career after taking a course in gilding and studying art history in Munich and Paris. A fan of Byzantine and medieval art, he was fascinated by the range of operations required for the restoration of gilded wood and discovered a love of working with three-dimensional objects. He found the tactility of the material particularly appealing.

Restoration requires detailed research, and it is not unusual for experts such as Youri to study similar objects in museums before setting to work. He works alongside his wife Anne, whose task it is to prepare each object meticulously for restoration. Once she has stripped off the layers of gilding, the piece can 'speak' and reveal its history. What lies hidden beneath these golden flakes tells her a lot about the place and period in which the piece was made and the form that any restoration should take. A restorer must remain faithful to the original style, and for this reason the initial stage of identifying and authenticating the object is perhaps the most demanding, requiring absolute accuracy. The key question is always how far to go in terms of repairing and replacing missing pieces, and this requires expert knowledge of joinery, woodcarving and casting.

During the process of gilding and regilding, it is essential to select the right colours. To this end, over the years Youri has amassed a collection of antique materials as well as tools from different historical periods. Since he set up the workshop in 1986, he has restored many prestigious pieces for museums and collectors, often carrying out the work in close cooperation with his clients. Examples of his craft include Marie Antoinette's monogrammed fire screen at Versailles and an early 18th-century console table designed by Joseph Effner, now housed at the J. Paul Getty Museum in Los Angeles.

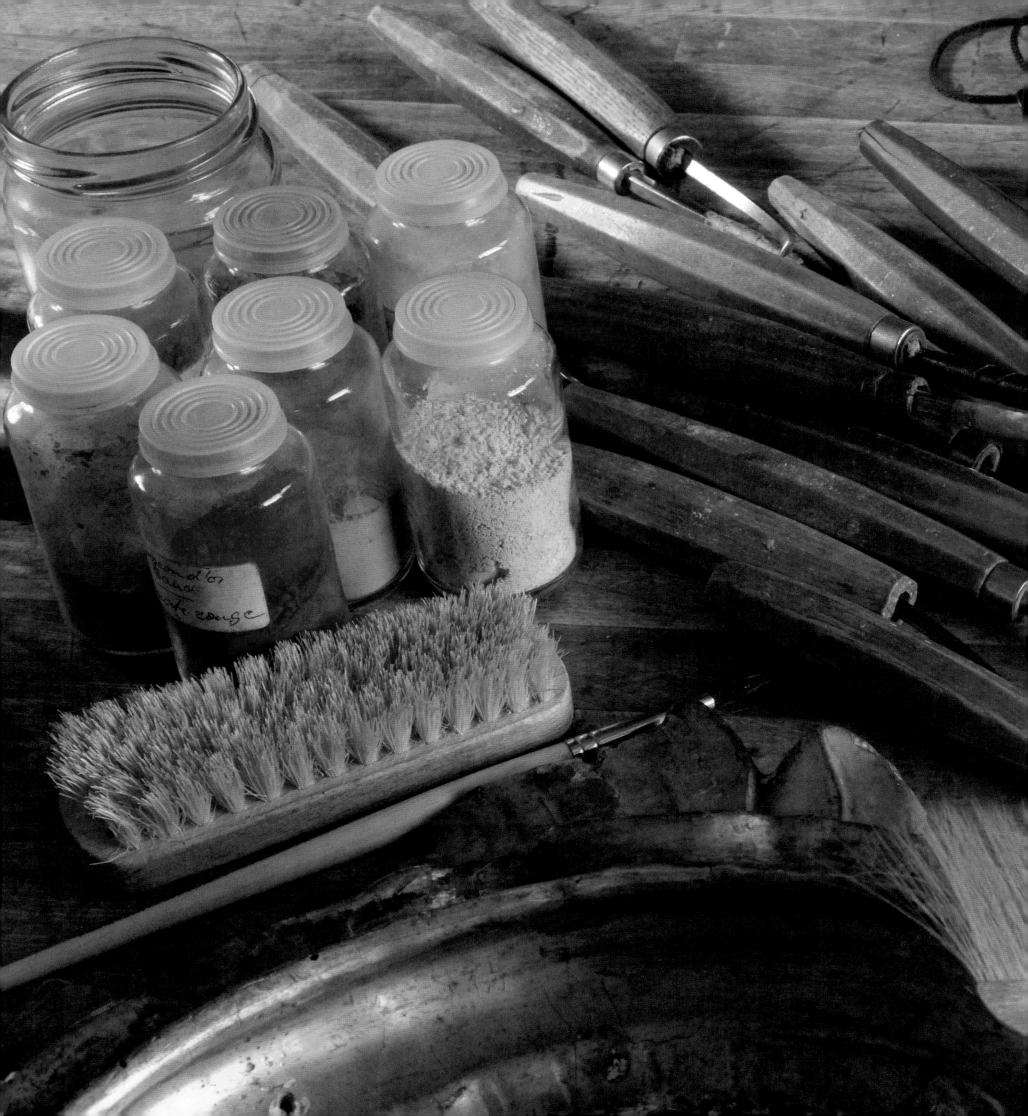

Marie Dubost

Gilder and restorer of gilded and painted wood

Having taught for several years, Marie Dubost decided to devote herself to the art of restoration. She learned how to restore paintings at the Beaux-Arts in Paris and spent several years completing her training in the United States. Although she wanted to stay in America long-term, she returned to France to specialize in gilding and has remained there ever since.

In 1992, Marie opened the Atelier de la Feuille d'Or, working with private collectors, dealers and prestigious institutions such as the Louvre and the Château de Chantilly. She sees herself as a diagnostician, applying her skills to painted and gilded wood rather than diseased bodies. She is able to detect the trials and tribulations that an object has undergone – what is broken and what can be repaired – and exercises infinite patience in getting to know the object before she starts. This is the hallmark of the skilled restorer: knowing whether a piece should be restored and how far to take any interventions.

Like all gilders, Marie has her own way of doing things. She holds a small cushion in the palm of her left hand, gripping it with her thumb. On the cushion is a gold leaf. Between her ring finger and her little finger she holds a brush with which she moistens the surface on which she is working. Between the middle finger and the ring finger she grips a long-bladed knife, perfectly balanced, with which she cuts her squares of gold. These are to be stuck on the wood, which has been coated with glue and Blanc de Meudon beforehand. In her right hand she holds the gilder's tip brush. This brush has a single row of bristles that create a build-up of static and pick up the gold leaf. She then wets the surface that is to be gilded and applies the gold leaf. Once it has dried, the gold leaf is polished with agate to make it shine in all its glory.

Like painters with their colours, gilders can only become masters of their craft when they have learned to make use of the different shades of light and dark. On a surface of smooth wood, the application of gold can be quite dazzling, whereas a rough surface will produce a matt effect. Understanding how to alternate and to harmonize these two qualities is what gilding is all about.

Simon-Pierre Étienne

ATELIER SIMON-PIERRE ÉTIENNE
Cabinetmaker and restorer of furniture and objets d'art

When Simon-Pierre Étienne was a child, he was surrounded by the curiosities of his family home: objects collected by his grandfather and great aunt, who were both antique dealers, and his father, an enlightened connoisseur whom the young Simon-Pierre used to accompany whenever he had a piece restored. It was only natural that the child should develop an eye and an instinct for the beautiful objects that have remained so integral to his life.

Simon-Pierre founded his workshop in 1980 and gets a huge amount of satisfaction from restoring the objects entrusted to him. He likens this task to a philosophy: a way of looking at objects and at the world with a code of ethics that demands the highest possible standards and the obligation to acquire a deep knowledge, not only of the history of art but also the expertise handed down by the greatest designers and artists of the past. One such designer is the French cabinetmaker André-Charles Boulle (1642–1732), who was granted royal favour from 1672 onwards and produced many of the finest pieces of furniture at Versailles. He is particularly known for his method of inlaying metal and tortoiseshell, known as Boulle marquetry, which was all the rage during the reign of Louis XIV.

The workshop is steeped in the culture of the 18th century, and each of the seven artisans who work there does so independently. They are all devoted to the art of restoration, while respecting the unique, intrinsic value of the objects in their care. The approach to restoration may have evolved over the years, just as the instruments for scientific analysis of every aspect of an object have also advanced, but the workshop remains firmly based on the foundations of Simon-Pierre's expertise, dedication and perfectionism. With clients all over the world, he is often called upon to give advice when collections are up for sale.

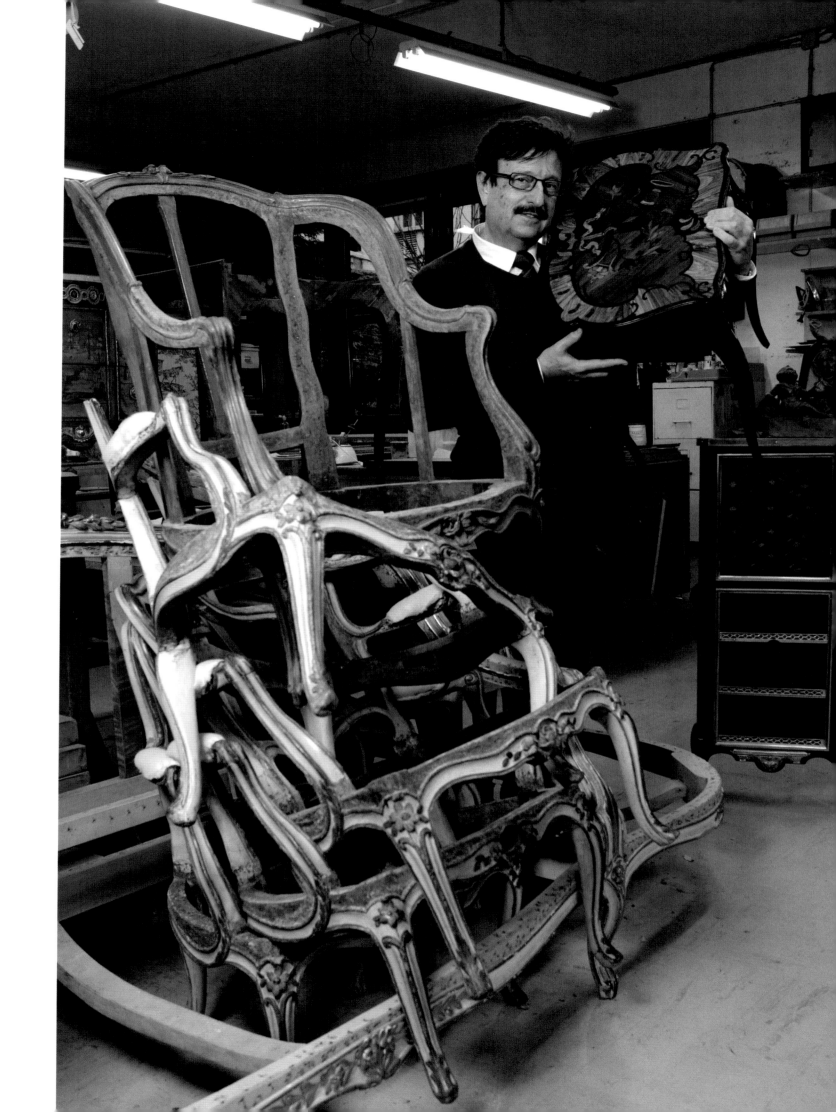

Sébastien Evain

ATELIER SÉBASTIEN EVAIN

Restorer of 18th-century furniture

Sébastien Evain learned his craft primarily from the great cabinetmaker Michel Germond (see page 9). From him, the young cabinetmaker acquired not only technical knowledge, but also discipline and respect for the furniture on which he works. Now with more than twenty years' experience, Sébastien exercises every aspect of this discipline in his workshop in Paris, designed especially for the restoration of furniture.

Disorder is an alien concept there: every object has its place. For each piece, he produces a thorough report detailing his interventions, accompanied by photographs. For example, during the restoration of a Louis XVI writing table, he wrote the following: 'The frame is made entirely of oak (apart from the top panel and the sliding shelf, which are in pine), and the marquetry depicts a swirling rosette on a bayadère background… The table has a built-in drawer on the right-hand side, which still has its original lock and screws. The four feet rest on their original castors.' By examining and analysing the traces left on the table by the tools of the original craftsman, he was able to confirm it as an authentic piece by the cabinetmaker Roger Vandercruse Lacroix, who enjoyed huge success in the 18th century, with commissions from the Garde-Meuble de la Couronne, the Duke of Orléans and Mme du Barry.

After thousands of hours spent studying and dissecting masterpieces, Sébastien is regularly called upon to give advice to collectors, to accompany them when they make their acquisitions, and to assist in the management of their collections. Everything he does is thoughtful, controlled and worthwhile, leaving us to wonder whether he is simply a passionate perfectionist in search of clarity and knowledge or perhaps represents a new generation of artisans whose work touches on the world of science.

Gwénola Le Masson

ATELIER L'AMARANTE
Restorer of painted furniture and other painted objects

Before devoting herself to restoration, Gwénola Le Masson applied her talent with colour and decoration to making up film actors. With the same intense concentration that she poured into creating the right cinematic image, she now focuses on recreating the authentic appearance of the objects she restores. With her sister Marie Dubost (see page 104), a gilder whose workshop is in the neighbouring court, she undertakes the restoration of furniture and other painted objects using traditional techniques and materials such as animal-skin glue.

Using solvents or scalpels to reveal the original colours that have disappeared beneath the patina of time or beneath more recent layers of paint, with meticulous care Gwénola uncovers the history of the object she is to restore. Some elements may be worn, faded or covered in grime. The aim is to bring the original paintwork back to life or to reconstruct it using traditional techniques, but she must also recreate the patina that reflects the effects of time and the signs of wear.

Most of the furniture and other objects that Gwénola restores date from the 17th and 18th centuries and come from private individuals, antique dealers, museums and collectors. She takes pleasure in breathing new life into these items – reviving the gentle bluish grey tints of a Louis XVI armchair, for example – and sharing in the history of the cabinetmakers, carvers and upholsterers who made them. The qualities of these artisans complement and mirror her own experience, research, expertise, sensitivity and intuition – all essential attributes in returning the objects to their former glory. Perhaps Gwénola's innate artistic sense has come down to her from her great grandfather on her mother's side, the painter Auguste-Michel Nobillet.

Rachida Mallogi

Restorer of antique tapestries

'I restore my tapestries as if I were restoring my own life,' declares Rachida Mallogi, who specializes in tapestries from the 16th to 18th centuries. The subject matter is usually taken from the Bible or Homer's *Iliad* and *Odyssey*, and the magic of the colours, the poses and the stories transports her 'as if touched by grace', she says.

Widely read, energetic and dedicated to her work, she reinforces her natural talent with her fine personal qualities. The tapestries come to her faded, damaged, full of holes, and she immerses herself in their stories and their histories in order to bring them back to life. In 1994, she was awarded the Meilleur Ouvrier de France for her restoration of a Gobelins tapestry.

Although self-taught, Rachida is recognized, respected and employed by all the major museums in France. Her list of clients includes the Musée National du Château de Pau, which houses the magnificent collection of Henry IV of France (1553–1610), and the Louvre. Her restoration of one 16th-century tapestry at the Musée Basque in Bayonne was the subject of a special publication. She also makes time to teach and train students, often taking them to see the treasures of her region at the Musée des Tapisseries in Aix-en-Provence and the Musée Grobet-Labadié in Marseilles.

Although she works alone in her workshop, which adjoins her home in Avignon, she is prepared to throw open her doors to those interested in her craft. In her own words: 'I know that education is above all an interweaving of views, and I like to get involved at the level of children and teenagers. When I welcome them to my workshop, or go and see them at their schools, or take them round a museum, I always like to drum it into them that there is no such thing as fate, that their destiny is in their own hands, and it can offer them a wonderful life.'

PRESERVING THE PAST   133

Fernando Moreira

Restorer of 17th- and 18th-century gilded bronze and cabinet work

'I'm a maverick,' Fernando Moreira admits with some relish, in the next breath insisting that he always wants to share ideas with others. It will already be clear, then, that this man is a complex but engaging character.

His father was a goldsmith in Fontainebleau and sometimes used to wake his children up in the middle of the night to show them beautiful objects. The workshop served as a playground for little Fernando, who did not want to disappoint his father and studied hard, but realized that what he really wanted was to feel the movement of materials and indulge in his passion for history. He turned his attention to conserving and restoring metals. He had already earned his pocket money by engraving, and could manipulate the goldsmith's tools as if they were coloured pencils. He worked in his father's workshop for a year and set up on his own at the age of twenty-five.

Bronze is his favourite metal because it is versatile and can be easily manipulated. Its uses were developed and expanded during the construction of the Palace of Versailles, which brought the goldsmith's work to the fore, largely due to the efforts of André-Charles Boulle. The beautiful pieces of furniture he created for Louis XIV are among the finest examples of 18th-century craftsmanship in the world. The king was also a great admirer of Italian art thanks to the influence of his godfather and mentor Cardinal Mazarin, who brought numerous Italian artists to France on his instruction. Their fine workmanship in bronze can be found throughout Versailles, for example in the light fixtures and furniture decoration.

Fernando has settled on the quays of the Hôtel de Ville in Paris, where since the early 2000s he has worked as a consultant for Christie's and Sotheby's, attending sales and advising private collectors. He is very selective about the works he takes on and is frequently moved by the sheer talent of the designers of the objects in his care. His role is often preventative as well as restorative, and he can never focus on more than five or six objects at a time. For this reason, he sees himself as a kind of aesthetic playboy because once a work has recovered its former glory, he swiftly moves on.

The discipline imposed by the quality of the object is reflected in the perfectionism of Fernando and the two colleagues who work with him in his workshop, one of whom is a cabinetmaker. The piece is the true source of his energy, and before approaching the task, he thinks in depth about what course of action needs to be taken. Modestly, he says it took him ten years to learn his craft, and another ten years to learn how to sell it. Now he is in demand from collectors, art dealers, museums and galleries, he is determined never to let them down.

Aude Vieweger de Cordoüe & Thomas Vieweger

ATELIER ARTIS

Sculpture restorers

Since they first met while studying restoration near Hanover in Germany, Aude and Thomas have shared a love for the restoration of sculptures, ranging from miniature to monumental. For more than twenty-five years, they have relished the daily challenge of seeking, finding and implementing the best solution for every problem. Restoration and conservation mean becoming subservient to the work, in order to stem the process of decay and reawaken the aesthetic impact of the original object, while keeping the restoration as accurate as possible.

Aude's main interests lie in the restoration of sculpture and furniture in her studio. A craft she has wanted to practise since she was fifteen years old, restoration is her true vocation. She has restored works by many well-known artists, including terracotta sculptures by Gervais Delabarre, a marble angel by Bernini, and many altarpieces, saints and madonnas as well as contemporary works.

In all cases, her adjustments and repairs must remain discreet, for the aim is not to recreate a piece but to protect and strengthen it, while remaining as close to the artist's original design as possible. She works with wood, terracotta (her favourite material), stone, marble, alabaster, plaster and polychrome objects. She also keeps records of her research into restoration processes and of each finished work.

While Aude's working day is spent in the studio, her husband travels the length and breadth of France, working on the cathedrals of Chartres, Amiens, Bordeaux, Troyes, Perpignan and Notre-Dame de Paris, among others. He also works on palaces and castles, town halls, small churches and chapels, and anywhere else where the skills of his team are required to clean sculptures, repair breakages, fill in gaps and make the artworks strong and secure. Recently they helped to restore the Grand Palais in Paris to its former glory, following a meticulous process of research and preparation. The project required a team of fifteen, working intensively for four years on a façade covering almost a kilometre.

Thomas's expertise is much in demand, and he is often asked to provide a preliminary study to explain why a restoration is required. He began by working on Romanesque and Gothic masterpieces, but his scope has since expanded to include more recent works as well.

For both private and public works, the Viewegers use high-tech tools to ensure that their work conforms to their strict code of ethics. Radiography allows them to examine a piece without causing any damage – they can study the way it was constructed, gauge the degree of damage, analyse the materials and layers of pigment, and thus determine precisely which repairs are needed. They use lasers to remove staining, and biomineralization to solidify stone that is beginning to crumble.

A particular source of pride is the restoration of Notre-Dame-la-Grande in Poitiers, a gem of Romanesque art from the 11th century, located just a few miles away from their workshop.

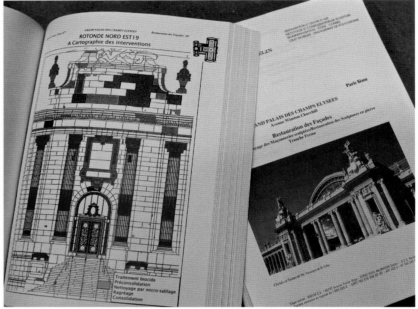

Élise Blouet-Ménard
Leatherworker

Jacques Bolelli
ATELIER SIMON MARQ – FORT ROYAL
Glass studio

Hervé Bruchet
ATELIER DARNE – FORT ROYAL
Gunsmith

Gérard Desquand
Heraldic engraver

Yves Dorget
VERRIER PÈRE & FILS
Passementier

Christian-Thierry Drevelle
ATELIER DREVELLE
Designer and cabinetmaker

Robert Jallet
Chairmaker and restorer

Patrick Fallon
Leatherworker

Reinhard von Nagel
ATELIER VON NAGEL
Harpsichord maker

Thomas Niemann
Artistic metalworker

Laurent Nogues
CRÉANOG
Printmaker and embosser

Nicolas Salagnac
ATELIER NICOLAS SALAGNAC
Medal engraver

CHAPTER 3

Living
Traditions

Élise Blouet-Ménard

Leatherworker

The sweet, tarry scent of Russian leather brings a touch of history to Élise's modern workshop, first opened in 2001. The material has a strong appeal to the senses, with its pungent scent and its tactile sensuality. There are thousands of different kinds of leathers, but when they are tanned in the traditional manner – in vats, with tree bark – each can be identified by its perfume, weight, suppleness, colour and even its sound.

After earning a Masters in cultural conservation and restoration at the Sorbonne, Élise went to the UK to train as a leatherworker. Initially, she was interested in metalwork, but found her true calling when she was asked to restore a suit of armour whose leather straps had corroded the metal, and decided to work with a tannery to produce a Hungarian leather whose chemical composition would not cause the metal to rust. A year of science studies and the fact that she attended a bilingual school gave her a solid background. Her aim was to work with her hands and to give full expression to her passion for art history. A year spent at the Leather Conservation Centre in Northampton reinforced her new vocation, for here she found an abundance of research material and a comprehensive approach to training that was not available in France. To recreate the leathers of different historical periods, it is necessary to know how they were made, although they exist in as many varieties as the animals and places from which they are derived. This information can be found in manuals such as those used by France's Guild of Leather-Sellers, founded in the 15th century. In this way, Élise was able to restore a cutlass (dating from 1833) and its sheath; the desk of Pope Pius IX, in red morocco embossed with gold leaf; Moynat and Goyard trunks belonging to late 19th-century travellers; wall panels of Cordoba leather for an 18th-century presbytery; and the cradle of the Prince Imperial Louis-Napoléon for the Musée Carnavalet. All of this was made possible by her comprehensive knowledge of the history of leathermaking.

Élise's order book is full of commissions from museums, collectors and private clients, and each one is special in its own way. While museums give her the chance to handle objects that are quite unique, people from the private sector bring her objects of personal, sentimental value.

She has only recently been invited to join the elite association of the Grands Ateliers de France, and is very excited at the prospect of getting to know fellow artisans whose specialities complement her own.

Jacques Bolelli

ATELIER SIMON MARQ – FORT ROYAL
Glass studio

The Atelier Simon Marq has been a centre of artistic excellence and technical expertise since 1640, and it promises to continue in the same manner long into the future. Through twelve generations, from father to son right up to the present day, the master glassworkers have passed on their knowledge and their talents. At the beginning of the 20th century, Jacques Simon set up the workshop in its present location, a few yards from Reims Cathedral, whose stained-glass windows he saved from the bombardments in 1917.

In addition to its contributions to religious heritage, in the late 1950s the studio, under the direction of Brigitte Simon and Charles Marq, took a new direction by working with some of the great contemporary painters. 'My circus takes place in the sky, it takes place in the clouds among the chairs, it takes place in the window where the light is reflected,' said Marc Chagall, in praise of the stained-glass window and the vision of the world that it offered. Georges Braque, Serge Poliakoff and Joan Miró followed the same artistic trail, and gave the stained-glass window an exalted place in the history of contemporary art. It is a history that continues to involve the artists of today: François Rouan, David Tremlett, Imi Knoebel, Hans Erni and Jean-Paul Agosti have all worked with Atelier Simon Marq.

In 2011, the atelier was bought by the Fort Royal group, which is committed to developing the many facets of this rich heritage in the fields of architecture, interior design, art and furniture. Jacques Bolelli, its director, discovered a passion for precious materials and craftsmanship when, in collaboration with the architect of the Bâtiments de France, he oversaw the restoration of the historic Fort National of St Malo, a building that has been in his family's possession since 1920. Indeed, it was the restoration of the Fort National – originally called the Fort Royal – that inspired Jacques to set up the group. But he is also thoroughly au fait with the contemporary world of communications and international exchanges. And so the workshop continues to evolve, responding to the demands of a new clientele, which includes the University of Columbia in the USA, a Hollywood star, and religious institutions all over the world. The current challenge, however, is an area of 350 square metres (3,750 sq. ft) – a chapel that forms part of a private college in the city of Reims.

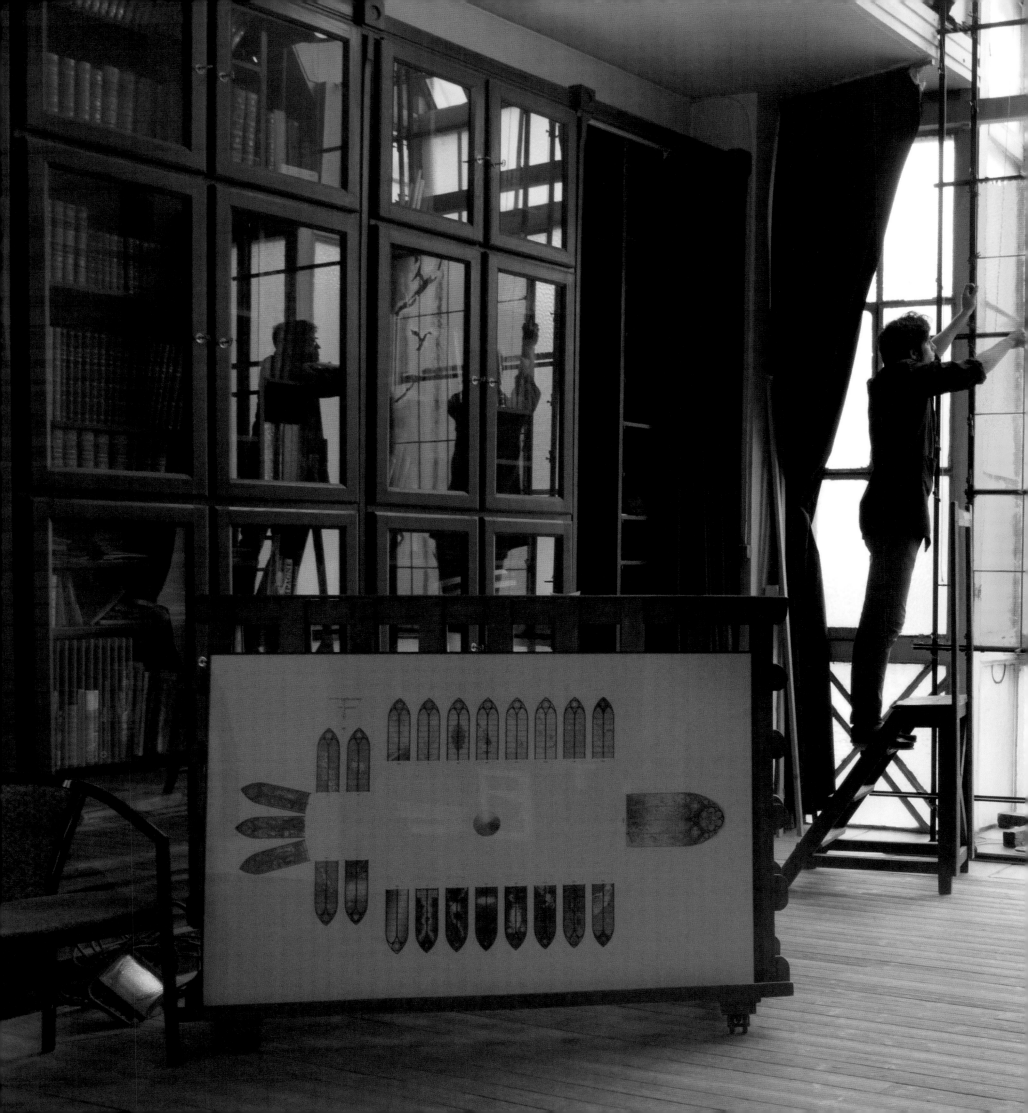

Hervé Bruchet

ATELIER DARNE – FORT ROYAL
Gunsmith

Comradeship and passion are central to the history of Atelier Darne. When Hervé's father took charge of the workshop, which was founded in 1881 by Régis Darne, he was surrounded by fellow craftsmen. Hervé, inspired by the spirit of craftsmanship, joined his father and took over the workshop in 1995. The atelier is now part of the Fort Royal group, whose president Jacques Bolelli – a man with a passion for guns and for outstanding craftsmanship – has given Hervé his backing to use the unique technique (perfected in 1900) that is applied to the manufacture of these 'guns that do not jerk', whereby the barrels remain fixed and only the breech moves and recoils.

In order to restructure the Atelier Darne, Fort Royal recruited a young member of an association called the Union Compagnonnique du Tour de France. Aymeric Suillerot is a graduate from the École d'Armurerie in Liège and another enthusiast for traditional expertise and the exquisite mechanisms that are the speciality of this workshop. Here, the pieces are assembled in the traditional manner, using machines of the period and methods in keeping with those of the gunsmiths, woodworkers and mechanics in an age prior to industrialization. The demands are comparable to those of high-end jewelrymaking or clockmaking.

The spirit of craftsmanship that characterizes the workshop is also reflected in the Atelier Darne's pride in sharing an expertise that is available to very few gunsmiths in the modern world. Those who are lucky enough to use these guns love the elegance of their form, their perfect balance, the reliability of their mechanisms, their ballistic efficiency, and the quality of their finish. The Darne gun is a hunting weapon of the highest class, and each one is made to measure.

Gérard Desquand

Heraldic engraver

Throughout the centuries, the role of the heraldic engraver has been to perpetuate family histories – a practice that reached a peak in the Middle Ages. Ironically, it is the history of Gérard Desquand's own family that got him into heraldic engraving in the first place. His father and grandfather passed down their own fascination with this art form – an inheritance that is evident in his own library.

Former student at the École Estienne in Paris, holder of Meilleur Ouvrier de France status and *maître d'art*: Gérard has a thirst for knowledge, like all members of the Grands Ateliers, but in his work with groups and associations – stemming from a desire to bring men and women together around their shared history – Gérard perhaps goes further than most. In fact, he now teaches engraving at his alma mater.

Gérard initially worked on signet rings, which gained particular popularity in the 19th century when, no longer the preserve of the rich, they started to be worn more widely. They often incorporated a seal, initials and a negatively engraved decoration, which imprinted in the positive in wax. Later, Gérard became fascinated with Mesopotamian cylinder seals – small, stone cylinders, invented around 3500 BC, whose surface was carved in intaglio with a design that left an impression when rolled in clay. The cylinders were used primarily as an administrative tool and, although often no more than a few centimetres in size, are seen today as important elements of social organization. They trace the history of humans before the invention of paper – a history that has been preserved because the material on which it was engraved has resisted the passage of time.

Fascinated by this heritage and its durability, Gérard set out to reproduce the ancient processes on metal. Moving from gold to brass, he now engraves cylinder seals of all sizes up to 20 cm (8 in.) in height, as if the preciousness of the material were of less value than the history it contains. And to continue this development to its logical conclusion, as a reflection – whether conscious or not – on the ephemeral and its eternal counterpart, he also creates the images of his cylinder seals on porcelain, which is perhaps the most fragile of all materials. With an almost metaphysical consistency, the subjects to which he devotes his work epitomize the fragility of nature and life. This was evident with his *Cylindre de la pérennité*, exhibited in Japan in 2013 and depicting Noah's ark – a picture of animals as well as humans, symbolizing both the continuity and the vulnerability of species.

Yves Dorget

VERRIER PÈRE & FILS

Passementier

Yves Dorget is the fourth generation of *passementiers* (makers of braids and trimmings) to work in this studio, which is located in the 20th arrondissement of Paris. He has run it successfully for more than twenty years, and if there is one watchword that characterizes his professional approach, it is 'humility'. He knows that in his particular craft, there is nothing new under the sun. It is so ancient, and the trimmings, gimps, braids and tiebacks have been produced in so many different forms, that no matter what variation you choose, it can never be original. What you must always remember is that every piece is no more than an adaptation inspired by the work of your predecessors. The important thing is to ensure that it is made with precision, care and minute attention to detail.

Yves is recognized internationally as an exceptional craftsman, and although many of his clients are French, others come from all over the world (the USA, the UK, Russia and Qatar, for example). They know that he can tackle the most intricate, complicated commissions, because his accumulated professional experience and his determination to achieve perfection in all his work enable him to meet any challenge. The basic principle is always to remain humble, to work hard, and to preserve the priceless satisfaction of a job well done.

Yves's workshop positively vibrates to the rhythms of the Jacquard perforated cards, which to weavers are the equivalent of sheet music to an orchestra. This is the last workshop of its kind still operating in Paris. Yves has more than ten assistants producing these delicate trimmings for various upholsterers, interior designers and antique dealers. Passementerie is a craft that can never dispense with handwork. There are certain types of skirt, fringe, ribbon and braid that simply cannot be produced industrially. They demand a degree of manual dexterity, precision and attention that machines cannot emulate. There are no schools of passementerie, so enthusiastic and conscientious artisans such as Yves Dorget are needed to keep this traditional craft alive.

Christian-Thierry Drevelle

ATELIER DREVELLE

Designer and cabinetmaker

The Drevelle family history would have been more straightforward if Thierry – born Christian, but rechristened at the request of one grand-mother – had followed in the footsteps of just one family member. The first generation of designers settled in Cognac during the 19th century. The second generation started off in Rue de Varenne in Paris. It was there that Thierry's uncle – a cabinetmaker – first introduced his sister to Thierry's future father, an interior designer. Both grandfathers were also immersed in the world of design, although all record of their work was destroyed in a fire.

As a child, Thierry had dreams of becoming a shepherd, but he changed his mind when he realized how hard and lonely it could be. Fascinated by his design roots, in 1973 he joined his uncle and father, who had opened their own workshop in Cognac in 1949. A dreamer like his father, but also a precise technician like his uncle, Thierry learned all about restoration and veneering first hand. After a few years, he decided to teach rather than practise these crafts. At the age of thirty, eager to learn more about the decorative arts, he enrolled at the École Boulle and attended classes run by the marquetry specialist Pierre Ramond.

He also set up his own space within the family workshop with his elder brother, who was responsible for the design, while Thierry focused on the manufacturing. When his brother died prematurely, Thierry took on a more creative role but also branched out into the cigar trade. His passion for cigars and love of travel took him to Cuba and the Dominican Republic, and he began to think up designs for cigar boxes. However, responding to the demands of his local area of Charente in southwestern France, an area famed for cognac, he produced crates to hold bottles of brandy, while continuing his work as a restorer.

Thierry is someone who throughout his life has never stopped learning. In 1999, a meeting with cognac house Hennessy marked a turning point for the workshop and for him personally. Since then, he has devoted himself almost exclusively to the creation of custom-made furniture, personalized cigar cases, and all sorts of decorative objects to serve as fittingly ornate accessories for luxury goods. He was artistic adviser in the construction of a storehouse for Martell cognac, designed resin sculptures to celebrate the bicentenary of Perrier-Jouët champagne and a special cabinet to mark the America's Cup jubilee, and devised a fascinating writing desk with concave front feet and convex rear feet – reflecting the idea that, in order to write, one must turn in on oneself, whereas the written word is for sharing. It should be mentioned that Thierry himself writes regularly, although he is keeping his work under wraps for the time being. His main concern at the moment is to develop a clientele for luxury goods in Hong Kong, where cigar lovers have found a truly exceptional partner in him.

Robert Jallet

Chairmaker and restorer

On the advice of an art history teacher at his college, Robert Jallet took the entrance exam and won a place at the École Boulle, where he discovered a very special craft: chairmaking. He learned all the basics of solid geometry – how to calculate the curves of armrests, backs and seats. This is a craft that covers all kinds of seating (chairs, folding seats, armchairs, sofas, beds) but also smaller objects such as console tables, candelabra, lecterns and screens. When making a reproduction of a piece, Robert always begins by recording all the details of the original, using tools such as a compass, set square, slide calipers, plumbline and spirit level, and then makes a working drawing that he can use as a template for his work. His workshop is full of these pieces of grey cardboard, covered with different notes.

Robert works with all sorts of wood, but particularly beech, a common material for chairs, and his tools include jigsaws, rasps, planes and spoke-shaves. He creates the basic structure but allows for different decorations, which he leaves to other specialists such as turners and carvers. Once the piece has been assembled, it then passes to other craftsmen who provide the cane or rush, varnish or patina, lacquer or gilding – and of course, the upholsterer, who finishes off the chair or sofa.

Robert opened his workshop in 1982, in the Bastille district of Paris, which has been a hub of furniture making for at least 300 years. Since the Bastille opera house was inaugurated in 1989, however, property prices have soared, and many of his fellow craftsmen have had to pack up and leave. As a result, his associates are often some distance away.

Robert's clients include antique dealers, collectors, designers and institutions, and they come to him to restore or make all kinds of seating: they might ask him to copy an old armchair acquired from a dealer or an auction, or call on him to create something entirely original. As the heir to a dynasty of artisans who worked with wood, Robert fears that the craft, as he practises it, is in danger of disappearing due to labour costs and technology that makes production quick but results in ephemeral products. Despite the long hours and an income that is probably nowhere near as high as it should be, his freedom and love of his work give him a feeling of wealth.

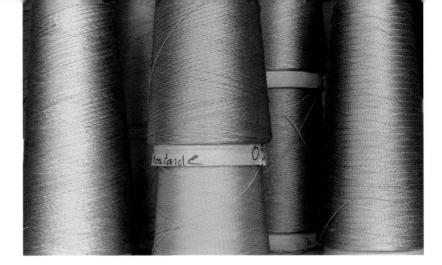

Patrick Fallon

Leatherworker

Any cigar case or miniature cigar box made by Fallon is likely to be in the hands of an adventurer, for they are designed to withstand any climate, from the Arctic to the Amazon. On a recent trip to Lapland, self-confessed adventurer and skilled leatherworker Patrick Fallon, who set up his workshop in 1984, tested cases covered with Orylag fur. He loves to lose himself in such isolated landscapes, which are a source of endless inspiration.

Fallon's catalogue contains some 700 items, each of which has its own story of adventure. The miniature cigar boxes, in addition to being waterproof, keep cigars fresh for several weeks in 70–75% humidity. These boxes are exquisitely covered, and the leather used for the lining is from Sherpa buffalo, which is also resistant to moisture. The cases are telescopic, and the interior leather is often orange – the colour of the company logo and reminiscent of the Swadhisthana chakra. In order that the smell of each case should be absolutely neutral, so that it can house the cigars without altering their particular perfume, the cases undergo a period of olfactory 'breaking in' – a process that takes seven days and involves using cigars whose function is to absorb the odours of the skins of the cases. These precious leathers are the skins of animals that have been specially bred.

Patrick's talents as a leatherworker were finely honed during three years he spent in Paris working for the Atelier Hermès, famed among other things for its leather bags. It was there that he met Serge Amoruso (see page 210), who not only became a lifelong friend but also introduced him to the pleasures of the cigar.

Patrick set up his workshop in Haute Savoie because he thought it would be a good place for his children to grow up. Sophie, his eldest daughter, spent a year in Australia but now works with him, and one day no doubt she will take over the firm. Charlotte, the youngest, has clearly inherited her father's love of the jungle and is planning to pursue her career as a photographer in Guyana in South America. As Patrick sees it, we should all have the opportunity to follow our dreams and fulfil our talents. That he puts this principle into practice is evident from his concern for the welfare of his collaborators and from Sophie's clear love of the craft.

Reinhard von Nagel

ATELIER VON NAGEL
Harpsichord maker

It must have been quite an adventure to rediscover a craft that had fallen into the black holes of history – harpsichord making. Throughout the 19th and most of the 20th centuries, it seemed that this instrument had been superseded by the far more powerful and versatile piano. There were tentative efforts to resurrect the harpsichord, but they led to an impasse: spurred on by musicians such as Wanda Landowska, the firm Pleyel altered the instrument in an attempt to improve it. In a way, this was a tribute to the industrial progress of the early 20th century, when the musical world imagined it was hearing the true harpsichord sounds of Johann Sebastian Bach, Jean-Philippe Rameau and other composers such as Girolamo Frescobaldi, although they were nothing like the original.

It was only during the second half of the 20th century that people began to make harpsichords that were as close as possible to those of the 17th and 18th centuries, with their lightness of touch and their richness of tone. Reinhard von Nagel was lucky enough to be a part of this tentative revival, and to be trained by Hubert Bédard and, especially, William Dowd, who went into partnership with him soon after they first met in 1971.

Reinhard grew up during the Second World War, initially to the sound of bombs falling on a German industrial town in the Rhine Valley, and subsequently to the sound of artillery in a village where his mother and her four children had sought refuge. He had little schooling. After the war, he was able to study classical languages at secondary school but, thanks to an enthusiastic headteacher, learned almost as much music as Latin and Greek. At seventeen, he was first violinist in the school orchestra, a highlight being a performance of *Carmina Burana* conducted by Carl Orff himself. He also attended evening courses, and during the holidays trained in metallurgy. His work as a welder paid for his studies at university, which were chaotic – simply learning for the sake of learning. In between courses in law, he did classical dancing and choral singing, as well as coming to grips with the painful truths of his own country's recent history.

He finally settled in France when he was twenty-five. Once there, he preferred the scents of wood reminiscent of his childhood to the academic pressures of the Sorbonne. After acquiring a small joinery not far from Saint-Germain-des-Prés, he met two clients who became personal friends: Alain Vian, a dealer in antique musical instruments, and Hubert Bédard, a harpsichord restorer at the Paris Conservatoire National Supérieur de Musique et de Danse, who was to help him take his first steps along the road to making harpsichords.

Miraculously, all Reinhard's chaotic studies began to make sense and to form a coherent pattern once he discovered the harpsichord: his knowledge of languages, law, arts and crafts, music and research. In 1972, he went into partnership with William Dowd. From the very first day, the research and the exchange of knowledge and newly acquired expertise became the driving force behind the workshop. In order to build and restore harpsichords, they needed to find the materials used by the old masters, their techniques, their terminology – in several different languages – their methods and their codes of practice. The sources on which Dowd and Reinhard drew were the old instruments themselves, the iconography, antique books and period compositions.

Today, harpsichords from different schools emerge from the workshop. Its sphere of influence has grown to international proportions: in 2013, nearly 1,000 harpsichords bearing the name 'William Dowd–Paris', 'Von Nagel–Paris' or 'Reinhard von Nagel' were being played in thirty different countries. The decoration of these harpsichords is a different field of research. The temptation would be to mimic the ornamentation of the old instruments, but reviving an ancient tradition does not necessarily mean aping it. Reinhard decided to imitate them in a different way, by turning to the painters of his own time – the likes of Marc Chagall, Pierre Alechinsky, Olivier Debré and Stefan Beiu, who combined their artistic genius with the expertise of Atelier von Nagel in a number of harpsichords.

Reinhard has taught at the Paris Conservatoire National Supérieur de Musique et de Danse, as well as at the Mozarteum University in Salzburg. In 1993, he was the co-founder of the first international harpsichord competition in Warsaw. From 2005 until 2008, he was president of the Grands Ateliers de France. In 1988 he was nominated as expert for the Court of Appeal in Paris, and in 1994 he was granted the title of *maître d'art*.

Thomas Niemann

Artistic metalworker

Thomas Niemann has been fascinated by metal for as long as he can remember. It was only natural that he should train for a career in iron and metalwork. Two people were instrumental in the development of his own style. The first was Cees Rombout, with whom he completed his training in the field of restoration. The second was the renowned Alfred Habermann, who took him under his wing and was key in helping him to find new ways of expressing his creativity. A love of contemporary work and a true gift for conservation are the legacy of these two master–pupil relationships.

After living in several different European countries (Germany, the Netherlands, Italy), Thomas decided to settle in France and for more than a decade has run his own workshop in Châteaurenard. Having enjoyed the privilege of learning first hand from master craftsmen, he was determined to pass on his own expertise and took on a pupil.

Thomas makes all his own tools, which are often the product of a particular kind of recycling – making pincers from car springs, for example, or a punch from a set of weights. It is quite normal for him to make suitable tools when he takes on a new project, which not only gives him the confidence that they will meet his exacting standards, but also allows him to work independently.

He loves to work the iron in his huge forge as if it were clay. In his expert hands, the metal curves, softens, undulates, but one of his many talents is the ability to exploit this flexibility while remaining faithful to the fundamental character of the material. These special gifts are recognized and admired by a clientele that includes architects, gallery owners and private customers.

Laurent Nogues

CRÉANOG
Printmaker and embosser

Laurent Nogues founded luxury design studio Créanog in 1994, with the aim of revitalizing the graphic arts. As is so often the case in the world of arts and crafts, the skills and knowledge that form the cornerstone of his business have been passed down from one generation to the next. When Créations Fournier – the printing company headed up by Laurent's father – was sold, the craft of embossing that his father had practised very nearly disappeared. On finishing his diploma at Olivier de Serres, Laurent found himself all alone in his quest to save it from extinction. Endowed with a good fighting spirit and a diploma in international trade, he rescued two embossing machines from the company and established the design studio.

The workshop now employs sixteen people engaged in design, fabrication and traditional embossing and découpage. Laurent has succeeded in recreating a company that designs and makes caskets, cases, maps,

brochures and display units for the world of luxury goods. At its heart is the art of graphic communication, combining traditional techniques such as engraving, embossing and hot stamping with the most contemporary visual tools. A series of privately sponsored guidebooks published by the Éditions du Patrimoine and dealing with La Sainte-Chapelle in Paris, Cluny Abbey, Carcassonne, and the Pantheon in Rome are a perfect example of this. In these books, embossing was used to give blind readers a better sense of the architectural gems to be found in these places, with detailed views of buildings and plans, for example, as well as more traditional descriptions in braille.

Laurent's greatest challenge has been to raise the profile of his craft and revive a demand that had almost died out. In 2011, his achievements in the field were recognized when he was awarded the title of *maître d'art*.

Nicolas Salagnac

ATELIER NICOLAS SALAGNAC
Medal engraver

In 1499, one of the first French medals was struck in Lyons to commemorate the visit of Louis XII and his wife, Anne of Brittany. Lyons is also the city that Nicolas Salagnac calls home – and he reckons it is not altogether a coincidence.

From an early age, Nicolas knew that he wanted to do something with his hands, something that involved drawing. Encouraged by his grandfather, a cabinetmaker, he enrolled at the École Boulle, where he was inspired by Pierre Mignot to become an engraver. In 1994, having already gained some experience in the world of work, he was approached by FIA, a subsidiary of A. Augis, to head up its engraving workshop in Lyons. Here, Nicolas familiarized himself with the whole range of techniques necessary for the art of medal engraving. A retired engraver named Claude Chaland, touched to discover a young man eager to carry on a tradition that had almost disappeared, gave him his tools, so that they might 'come back to life in his hands'. Nicolas also got to know Claude Cardot, who had achieved the status of Meilleur Ouvrier de France in 1972 and did freelance work for the company. This was an important contact for Nicolas, who has the greatest respect for this renowned engraver and medal maker.

In 2000, Nicolas was also awarded the title of Meilleur Ouvrier de France and set up his own engraving workshop three years later. The process of engraving is long and painstaking, with each stage carried out entirely by hand using traditional tools and techniques. It is highly detailed work that obliges him to spend hours and hours focused on just a few millimetres at a time. He specializes in medals but also makes trophies, and it gives him great satisfaction to create objects to celebrate achievements or to be given as coveted gifts. Among his designs are the official medal for the President of the French Republic, the medal of honour for the Villa Medici in Rome, and various commissions for the city of Lyons. These are then minted by Pichard-Balme, Arthus-Bertrand or the Monnaie de Paris, for example.

In an age when the world is dominated by consumerism and standardization, Nicolas affirms with each of his creations that 'only man is capable, through his skill and precision, of inscribing meaning into matter and arousing emotions, and imparting sensitivity, vision, spirit, soul.'

Serge Amoruso
SERGE AMORUSO DESIGN
Leatherworker

Gilles Chabrier
Glassworker and engraver

Pierre Corthay
CORTHAY BOTTIER
Men's shoemaker

Sylvie Deschamps
LE BÉGONIA D'OR
Embroidery artist

Caroline & Tristan Fournier
Sculptors and model car makers

Yves Gaignet
Model ship builder

Dragui Romic & Arnaud Paix
ATELIER EDGARD HAMON
Costume jewelers

Michel Heurtault
Maker and restorer of umbrellas and parasols

Françoise Hoffmann
Felt artist

Fanny Liautard
Haute couture designer

Catherine Nicolas
Lacquer artist

Nelly Saunier
Plumassière (feather artist)

Alain de Saint-Exupéry
Locksmith

Jean-Luc Seigneur
Engraver and embosser

Pietro Seminelli
Textile designer

Christian Thirot
ATELIER CHRISTIAN THIROT
Restorer of scientific instruments and glass engraver

CHAPTER 4

Unique and Unusual

Serge Amoruso

SERGE AMORUSO DESIGN
Leatherworker

Serge Amoruso believes in keeping an open mind, pushing boundaries and making his own dreams. Driven by an insatiable curiosity, he seizes every opportunity that comes his way – whether it is immersing himself in reading the works of the great psychoanalysts or teaching children with learning disabilities. He pours all these qualities into his work with leather, a highly versatile medium that can be combined with all sorts of materials, from ivory to rosewood.

At seventeen, he trained with Hermès, in the workshop that makes the famous bags. His father was a cabinetmaker, but Serge's fascination was with leather rather than wood. He mastered the techniques of leatherwork that would enable him to turn his hand to any task, from sewing a piece of shagreen by hand to making bespoke objects for high-end brands. As well as certain indispensable flagship products such as wallets, suitcases on wheels, handbags and cigar cases, he creates unique luxury items. One

example is a case for a Fabergé egg: conceived as a single piece and digitally designed to achieve the perfect cut, the case was almost like a sculpture. The same is true of the leatherwork he designed for a lift in Monaco, another one-off creation.

Whatever he is working on, Serge gives it his all. Everything is done by hand to the nth degree of perfection in the simple little workshop where Laurène – a former apprentice who is now independent – has been working for ten years, along with a young apprentice and Serge's wife Michelle, who helps with the administrative side of the business. Serge's tools are simple – hammers, sewing machine, a machine to cut and thin the leather – and the secret lies in the art of cutting. The sewing is done by hand from the open side, which requires a vast number of stitches; a wallet alone is composed of forty pieces. To finish an item off, in keeping with every other fine detail, the leather is painstakingly polished.

Gilles Chabrier

Glassworker and engraver

Sand is the raw material of the glassworker, whose task it is to decide the quality of the grain and the intensity of the jet. When shapes cut directly into blocks of glass turn into sculpted faces, it is as if we see a work of art emerging and all the technical processes that went into creating it seem to disappear before our very eyes.

Gilles has his own technique of sandblasting, which he inherited from his father and grandfather before him, whose workshop – founded in 1928 at the Bastille – worked on the decorative glass for the steamship *Normandie*. Gilles is known in particular for his glass heads. In his skilful hands, glass takes on a magical aura, whether it is polished or sanded, flat or curved. His sensual sculptures tell their own story and reflect the human soul in all its complexities, channelling our joy, our sadness, our rage, our calm.

He also makes furniture, lamps, mirrors and decorative objects out of glass. He relishes the challenges set him by architects and designers, and his workshop is like a laboratory from which there emerges one unique creation after another. Nowadays, he incorporates luminescence into his works, so that they are as dazzling by day as they are by night. He also has many monumental pieces to his credit, including a sculpture in Morzine to commemorate ski racer Jean Vuarnet's victory at the Olympic Games in 1960.

Gilles is a man of many talents and can be just as expressive when he uses his sandblasting techniques on other materials such as marble, wood and metal. Today, his son Vincent works by his side, and so we can rest assured that this unique expertise will not be lost.

« Un général qui a compris l'essence de la guerre est l'arbitre de la destinée de son peuple, il détient entre ses mains la stabilité de la nation. »

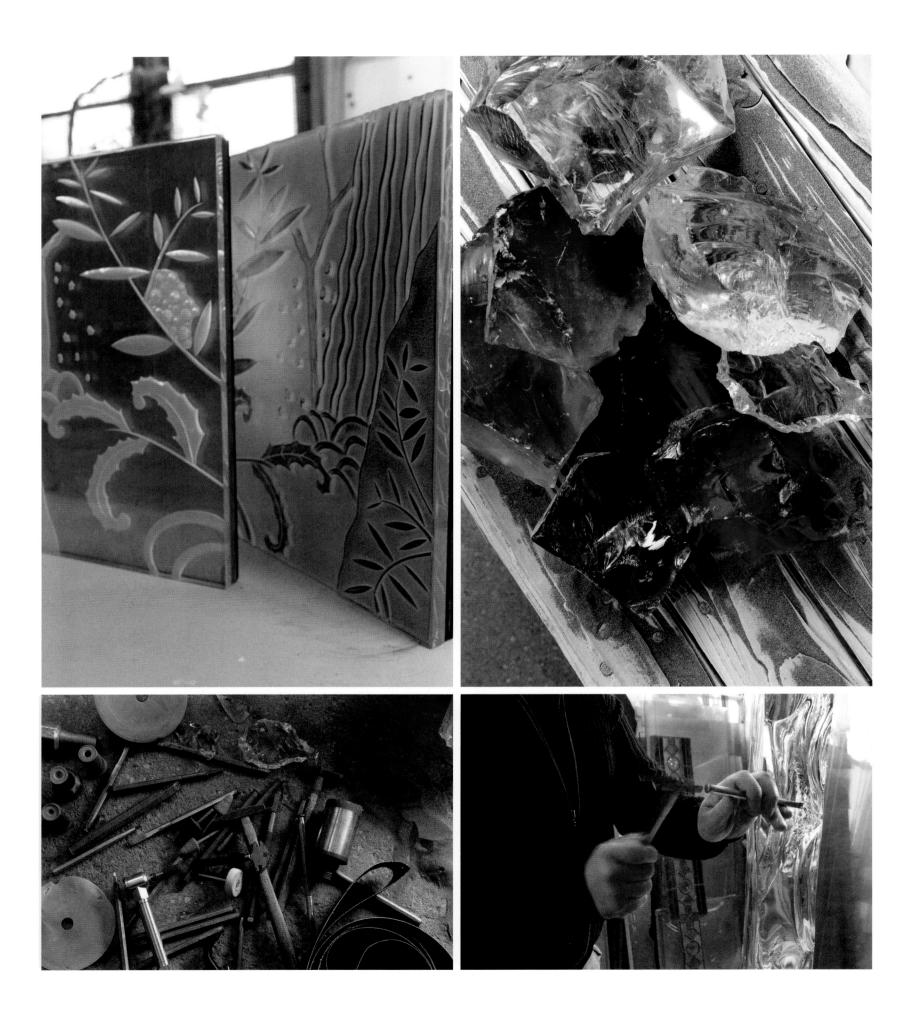

Pierre Corthay

CORTHAY BOTTIER
Men's shoemaker

Pierre Corthay's first source of inspiration was his grandmother's cousin, Valentine, who was an extraordinary avant-garde artist. Her atelier was close to Pierre's school, and as a little boy, he used to stop and gaze in wonder at the furniture, sculptures and other marvels she had designed. Even her doors were lined with leather.

Although Pierre's actor parents were quick to recognize the talents of a boy who was more interested in tools and workbenches than in childhood games, credit is surely also due to his spiritual godmother Valentine, who inspired the young apprentice to go and see how things were done by the experts. Back in the 1980s, only saddlers and shoemakers could instruct him in the arts of leathercraft. His career was shaped by the idea of combining the pleasures of sculpture with the work of transforming leather into shoes: 'You should be able to look at a shoe from all angles, as you would a sculpture.' The dream of becoming a luxury shoemaker rapidly became an obsession. He was soon joined by his younger brother Christophe, and the workshop they opened in the early 1990s swiftly expanded, but their mission has never changed: designing the most beautiful men's shoes. They are only made for men because Pierre claims that women would not have the patience to wait for a perfect pair of ankle boots or pumps.

The business could easily have remained on a small scale, making 150 pairs a year, but Pierre has always had bigger ambitions. First of all, Lanvin commissioned him to produce a collection of ready-made footwear. Then in 2000, Robert Rubin, American economist and former director of Goldman Sachs, ordered fifty made-to-measure pairs for members of his private golf club. The business found itself expanding once more. Today it is a major company, with Maison Corthay stores around the world: in Tokyo, London, Hong Kong and Dubai. Corthay shoes can also be found at Harrods and Selfridges in London, Saks in New York, and in Beverly Hills and San Francisco. Pierre remains artistic director, and worldwide the company employs forty-five people.

Sylvie Deschamps

LE BÉGONIA D'OR
Embroidery artist

When Sylvie Deschamps first arrived at Bouvard & Duviard in Lyons, it was love at first sight. Here was a company where you could still breathe in the scents of the 19th century, where the floorboards creaked. It was also where the young Sylvie learned everything she needed to know about the craft of embroidery from her mentor Lucie Teston, who was deaf and imparted her knowledge by gesture alone. Sylvie, who had always had a gift for drawing, had just done her certificate of embroidery at the Lycée de Rochefort, imagining that she would now be entering the world of lace and lingerie. Although initially she was limited to sewing patterns for flags, pennants and capes, the moment she started working with gold thread, she was infatuated. She also learned restoration. When the company was sold and moved to the Loire, Sylvie – now a young woman – was invited to direct the workshop, but she did not like the idea of living in the village of Noirétable, high above sea level.

At this point, fate stepped in. The head teacher at the Lycée de Rochefort, Marie-Hélène César, now president of the association of Le Bégonia d'Or, asked her to run a course for a diploma of embroidery, which in turn led to her becoming director of this embroidery workshop. Sylvie still runs the workshop, together with César, *maître d'art* Marlène Rouhaud, and a secretary-cum-assistant who does much of the preparatory work. For example, every piece of embroidery begins with a design drawn on tracing paper, and the outline of this is perforated so that the design can then be transferred to the material with zinc white (the outline then disappears beneath the embroidery).

The cannetilles, between 80 and 90 centimetres (31–35 in.) long, are cut to the desired length and then threaded like beads and sewn onto the material. Sylvie, who was given the title of *maître d'art* in 2010, buys her most important material, her gold thread, from another *maître d'art*, Daniel Gontard, of the Établissements Carlhian in Lyons. Braids, threads and sequins are all used for haute couture and decoration, as well as for restoration. The work covers all kinds of objects: cushions for Angélique Buisson, an interior designer based at Thonon-les-Bains; heels and soles embroidered in 24-carat gold thread for a pair of Massaro pumps; the back of a Philippe Starck sofa in gold-embroidered leather.

Sylvie never tires of inventing new things and enjoys contributing to the work of various contemporary artists. She embroidered photographic paper for Laurent Moriceau and coloured snowflakes for Martine Aballéa. The actor Philippe Noiret, a faithful client of the great shoemaker John Lobb, also commissioned her to embroider his gold monogram on several pairs of luxury slippers.

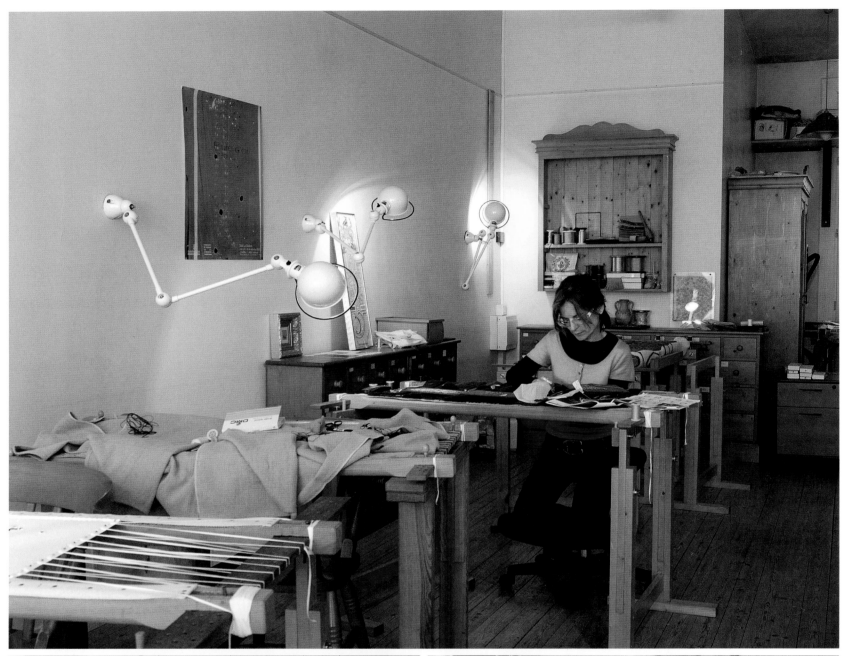

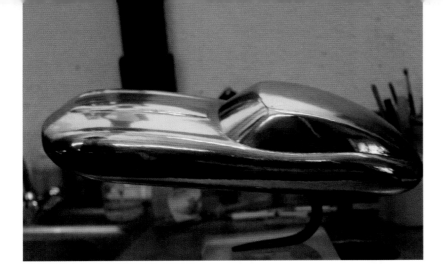

Caroline & Tristan Fournier

Sculptors and model car makers

Caroline and Tristan Fournier were made for each other. She has been repairing cars ever since she can remember, and he has collected every miniature model he could find: he now owns over a thousand. Both of them are passionate about constructing the finest models of the world's finest cars.

They trained in sheet metal craft, leathercraft and cabinetmaking, and then decided to set up their own atelier. A friend who was a Ferrari dealer in Clermont-Ferrand encouraged them to make a Ferrari Daytona, the legendary red car that won every major race during the 1970s. They made an appointment with Pozzi, the well-known importer, and while they were waiting to see him, another client who was waiting asked them what model of Ferrari they had. Caroline calmly replied that they had a Daytona Group 4. The gentleman went to the window to look for it in the car park, but then to his surprise saw the car, on a 1:8 scale, being taken out of a cardboard box that had once contained soap. Racing driver Alain Prost was the next to arrive and admire the model. A few days later, he posed with it for some of the most famous international magazines. He suggested that Caroline and Tristan should make a model of the F40, using the same revolutionary materials as the real thing: carbon fibre and Kevlar. A few weeks later, following an exhibition at the Salon Rétromobile, they received their first commission and went to the Ferrari headquarters in Italy, where they were entrusted with the plans for the F40. This was a new challenge, because unlike other models with metal bodies, the F40 had to be made piece by piece and the body had to be injection-moulded from carbon fibre and Kevlar. When you realize that a windscreen wiper alone consists of fifteen parts, it is not hard to imagine what a huge amount of work was involved in constructing the complete model. While Caroline made the individual pieces, some of them in wood, Tristan designed and shaped the bodywork. Each model took 2,500 hours to make.

More recently, the two of them embarked on a brand-new adventure: a model Bugatti T22, dating from 1914. The mudguards, dashboard and floor were of varnished mahogany, the brass accessories were plated with 24-carat gold, the seat was lambskin, the hood lined with leather, and the red rear lights were Swarovski crystal. No expense is spared when clients turn to Caroline and Tristan to make their motoring dreams come true.

Yves Gaignet

Model ship builder

Yves's workshop is covered with plans and sketches of ships, hulls, sails and pulleys. The call of the sea came to him from two directions: a grandfather who was a Cape Horner, and the maternal side of the family, who traditionally attended the École des Beaux-Arts in Paris. The family had always owned pleasure boats, and Yves sailed as a child. In his teens, he spent his school holidays on ships. It was this love of life on the ocean wave that ultimately led to his vocation – making model ships for display in living rooms or libraries – although initially the thought of becoming an artisan didn't even cross his mind: he started out as a sailor, driven by a desire for the exotic and a taste for new sights and sounds in distant lands, and inspired by the works of Joseph Conrad and Herman Melville. When Yves carved some model hulls and sold them, his career path was set.

This brilliant artisan taught himself by studying ships in the tiniest detail – the shape of the hull, the figurehead, the subtle linear forms of masts and ropes, the gloss… Ships require a lot of upkeep, and during the long voyages he learned to do all kinds of odd jobs, building up his knowledge through practice. As he matured, he transformed all this experience into a very different form of navigation, because his commercial success in carving his model hulls led to a commission from the Musée National de la Marine in Paris: he was asked to build a model of the three-master *Belem*, originally built as a cargo ship and launched in 1896. Yves had already made a model of the *Paul Ricard*, in which Éric Tabarly had broken the record for crossing the North Atlantic on a sailing vessel in 1980. Now he began to receive major commissions both at home and abroad, from the Yacht Club de France, the Royal London Yacht Club, the New York Yacht Club and the Atlantic Yacht Club.

The model ships Yves creates are like an invitation to sail because they transport you in your imagination. Although he may be caught up in the art of miniaturization, his main pleasure still lies in the real thing. His techniques are sometimes borrowed from those of jewelrymaking, but when he is restoring models, he is lost in admiration and respect for the technical skills of the past, when the materials were no doubt valued more highly than the craft. Today he continues to sail the oceans in his imagination through the ships he reproduces, as well as on his own boat, the *Sauvage*. Twelve metres (39 ft) long, it was built in the United States in 1938 and symbolizes perfectly all the charms of New England during this era.

Dragui Romic & Arnaud Paix

ATELIER EDGARD HAMON
Costume jewelers

All day and sometimes all night, the workshop is buzzing with creativity. Dragui, Arnaud and their staff are preparing for Paris Fashion Week, when this season's ready-to-wear and haute couture collections are presented. During the runway shows, the great names of the fashion world may call on them at a moment's notice to provide a new accessory. And ever since it was founded in 1919, the Atelier Edgard Hamon – housed in the heart of Paris in a building designed by Gustave Eiffel – has answered the call.

The atelier originally made buttons for boots and gaiters, then added shoe buckles when the actress Mistinguett made them fashionable in the 1920s. When Coco Chanel brought trousers for women into fashion, these required belts, which in turn needed decorative buckles, as beautiful as any piece of jewelry. The artistry of the *parurier* or costume jeweler is measured by the degree to which it can match the concepts provided by great couturiers. Today this atelier works with metal and leather, and this unique combination of jewelry and leatherwork has become its trademark.

Leather is the speciality of Dragui Romic; she first came to Paris to study, and has worked at the atelier for twenty-two years. Jewelry has been the province of Arnaud Paix for the last ten years. Both of them liaise with designers, who come to them with sketches and ideas at various stages of completion. Dragui and Arnaud advise, consult and plan, calling on their expertise in handcrafted techniques, before producing a prototype using the chosen materials. This, they say in one voice – and it's easy to see that they are used to working as a team – is the most exciting moment. After that, the atelier gets to work. There is a staff of around thirty, including ten artisans, and all of their talents must be combined to fulfil each order. Dozens of pieces are usually produced, sometimes in a range of colours.

The workshop is a veritable Ali Baba's cave, holding a treasure trove of multicoloured leathers, ribbons and stones. The outstanding quality of the atelier's work is borne out by the fact that Jean Bergeron, founder of the Grands Ateliers de France (see page 10), took over the company in 2000.

Michel Heurtault

Maker and restorer of umbrellas and parasols

Before the door even opens, the sheer poetry of the window display is enchanting. The shimmering silk and billowing lace of the parasols and umbrellas are like something from a fairy tale. Entering the workshop, which nestles beneath the magnificent archways of the Viaduc des Arts in Paris, is like entering a painting by Seurat or Monet. Taffeta, lace and ribbon vie for attention with gold and silver pommels and handles of carved ivory, shagreen and exotic wood.

Michel Heurtault is self-taught and an avid historian. Originally a collector, he went on to become a historical costumier, then a restorer, and finally a designer of parasols and umbrellas. His ambition is to give new life to the art of umbrella making and to restore this neglected craft to its rightful place of honour. Once considered a mainstay of the French luxury industry, it is a field that is now almost completely industrialized.

Michel's craft requires a meticulous handling of materials. Having been a costumier since the age of eighteen, he is unique in his mastery of many traditional techniques, and today he is a leading light not only in the world of arts and crafts, but also in haute couture. He has worked for legendary fashion houses including Dior, Yves Saint Laurent and Hermès, while the support of renowned costume designers such as Danièle Boitard, Olivier Bériot and Anthony Powell has enabled him to indulge his great passion for history.

Michel's exceptional expertise, his combination of aesthetics and practicality, his mastery of materials, his control of light and shade, and every detail of his exquisite craftsmanship all combine to convey a symbolic message: what the modern world needs is a revival of the love for luxury. With the poetic lyricism of his work, he certainly practises what he preaches.

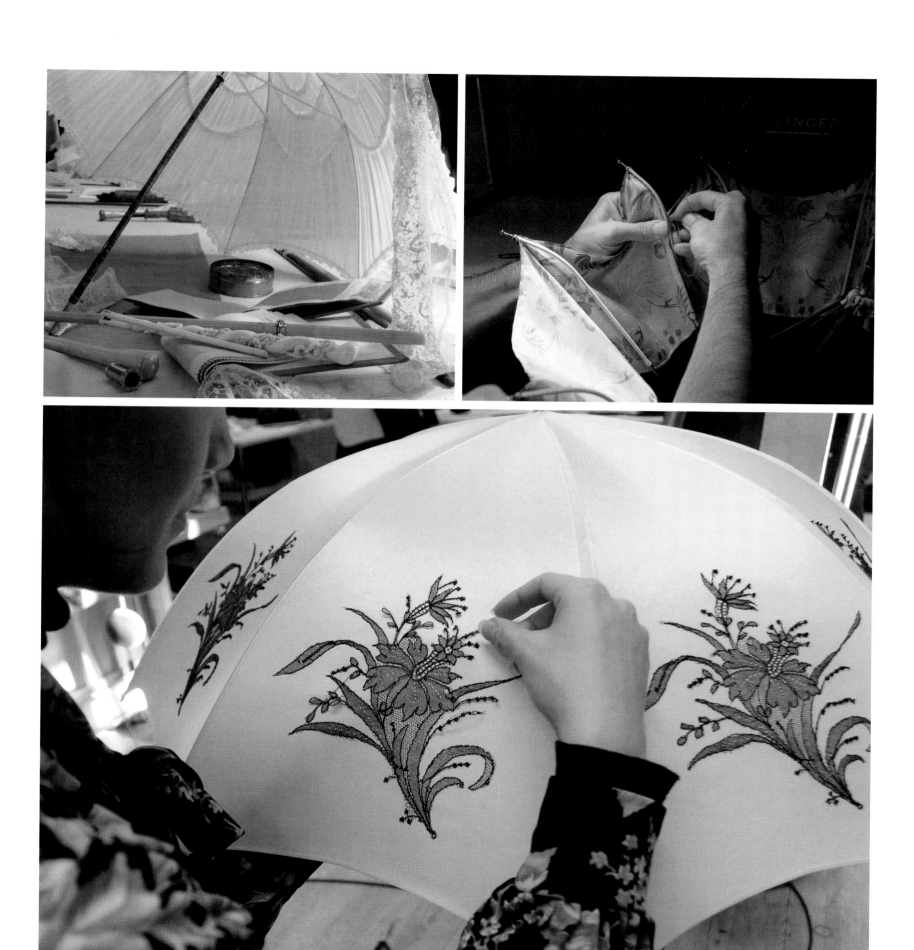

Françoise Hoffmann

Felt artist

Françoise Hoffmann positively bubbles with enthusiasm and imagination, and the sparkle in her eyes gives an immediate clue to her personality. She is a theatre person, and the theatre is both her passion and her profession. She first began to practise her craft of felting in the mid-1990s and has since created countless pieces for characters on stage.

Françoise started out making hats – once an important industry in her home town of Lyons – and trained in the workshop of the Musée du Chapeau in Chazelles-sur-Lyon. But her real delight is working with sheep's wool, from which the felt is obtained. The raw wool is washed and carded, and from a mixture of water and elbow grease this unique fabric finally emerges. As there are some 500 species of sheep in Europe alone, each animal differing according to its environment and feeding habits, there are some 500 varieties of fibre to play with. Getting to know the different sheep and wools requires a great deal of laboratory-based research, since fabric and style must be made to harmonize. Françoise's creations are accompanied by meditations on the passage of time, change and discovery. The clothes and decorative objects she makes are of tangible materials, but they grow out of the stories she tells herself as she observes the world around her.

Her felt is in high demand, from New York to Hue in Vietnam, for exhibitions and studies of the fabric. Her creations are sold in stores, some of which work in association with art galleries such as Artefact in Lyons, La Boutique Extraordinaire in Paris, and Julie: Artisans' Gallery in New York. With her typically free spirit, she delights in designing clothes without seams, and carpets (of more rustic materials) with very obvious seams. Françoise is a *maître d'art* and an intrepid traveller who draws endless inspiration from the images and ideas she finds in different places.

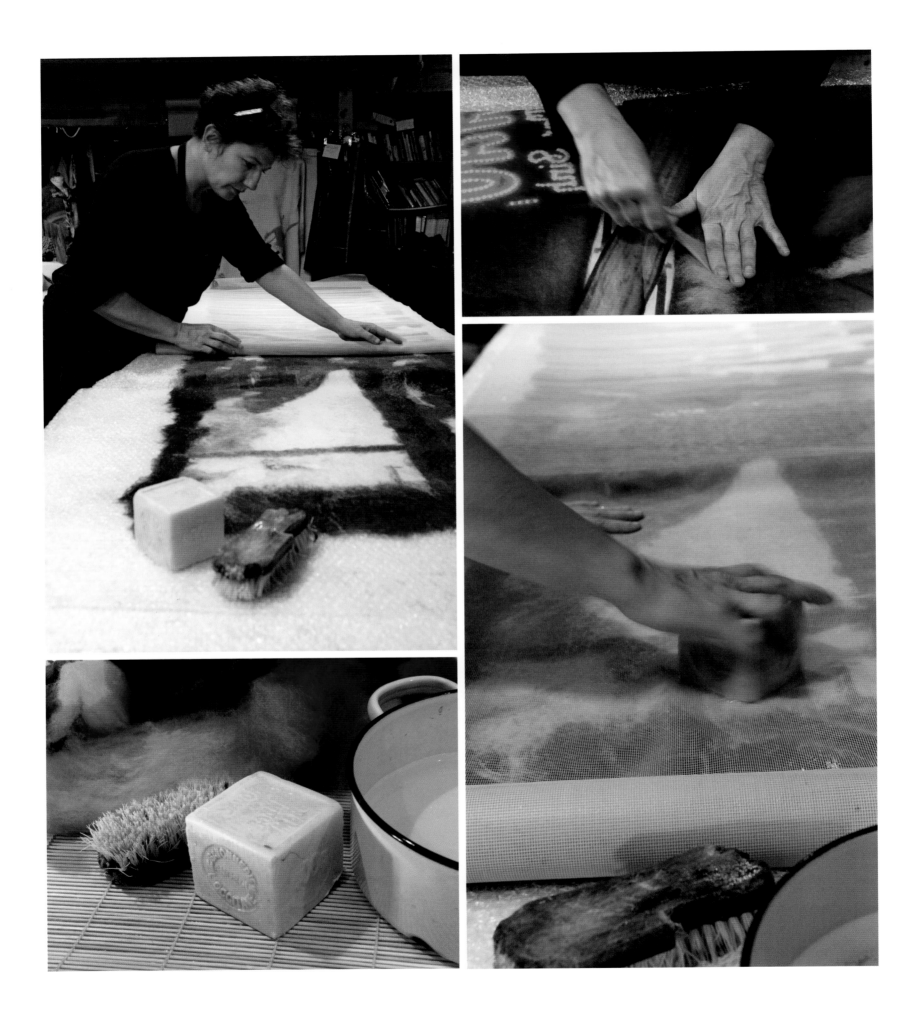

Fanny Liautard

Haute couture designer

The moment Fanny Liautard opens the door to her studio in Paris, near the Place de la Concorde, you are struck by the aura of feminine grace and elegance. Huge bunches of white roses and crystal candelabra stand on the mantelpiece of a room whose dimensions and decor are in the style of Haussmann. From a very early age, Fanny knew that she was an 'artist' – all she wanted to do was write, paint and sculpt. But it was an article she read when she was still in her teens that led her to her true vocation, despite a distinct lack of enthusiasm within her family. Haute couture, as the most sensual of the arts, enabled her to fulfil all her artistic dreams.

After training at the Chambre Syndicale de la Couture Parisienne, Fanny began her career in the fashion workshop of Hubert de Givenchy. She helped to create couture, ready-to-wear and lingerie collections, before setting out on her own in 1985. She loves loose-fitting garments and the use of bias binding to give the illusion of liquidity and airiness as the materials dance to the movements of the women they clothe – an image that calls to mind the fluid grace of American dancer Isadora Duncan.

Fanny's dresses are made for life's special occasions, or for film stars and opera performances. Her favourite materials are silk crêpe, chiffon, and Chantilly or Calais lace. Everything, from the design to the finishing touches, is done in her workshop, in collaboration with Manith, who has worked with her for the last twenty years. Embroiderers, pleaters, *plumassiers* and jewelers are also part of the team.

In order to create the dress of her client's dreams, Fanny must get to know her and discover her secret, most intimate desires. 'I must capture the thread of her feelings, the poetry of her individuality,' she says. Although most clients are brides-to-be, she points out with a twinkle in her eye that you can wear a pretty dress without needing to get married, perhaps revealing a hint of nostalgia for a time when festive occasions were less of a rarity.

Catherine Nicolas

Lacquer artist

Catherine Nicolas loves traditional techniques and one-off pieces, and is always searching for new ways of using lacquer to create works that suit contemporary tastes. Lacquer can be applied to surfaces both small and large, adorning jewelry, furniture, sculptures or other decorative items. Catherine's parents had the foresight to send her to study in Paris at the École Supérieure d'Arts Appliqués Duperré, an investment that paid handsome dividends, as it was there that she discovered no less than thirteen different crafts, including lacquerwork. Named as a Meilleur Ouvrier de France in 2006, she worked for ten years in advertising, where commerce and creativity sometimes make for uneasy bedfellows. It was during this period that she first travelled to Asia, where she experienced something she would never forget: the true art of lacquerwork. At college she had only ever seen lacquer applied with a spray gun, but when she visited Asian workshops, she discovered the basic techniques of urushi (vegetable lacquer), the traditions and techniques used in each country, and the skills of the men and women still practising this dying craft by hand. This journey proved to be her turning point.

She also set out to break down some barriers, respecting tradition but at the same time giving it a contemporary slant. To do this, she has developed her own unique styles of urushi and other ancient techniques. One of these is the Japanese technique known as *kintsugi*, a method of fixing broken ceramics together with glittering lines of gold lacquer resin. According to the tenets of Zen philosophy, the visible 'life' of an object takes precedence over 'perfection' and creates strength – hence these golden enhancements. *Kintsugi* endows an object with a sense of its own being by giving it new life. This form of restoration is in total contrast to European traditions, in which repairs are generally done as discreetly as possible.

Like its owner, Catherine's workshop is the embodiment of calm. It includes a large room where she works on large pieces, and another smaller one for smaller objects. Although she loves using lacquer on objects of all sizes, she is also interested in other traditional forms of decoration: eggshell inlay, mother-of-pearl, gold dust, gold leaf, engraving, relief. Catherine's lacquerwork is perhaps most notable for her experiments with unusual materials, such as inlaid newspaper, ceramics, ebony, horn or metal.

Most of her works are made smooth and glossy by sanding and polishing, which brings out the full glory of the colours. The many layers of lacquer allow inlays, hollows and reliefs to be created, giving each piece a unique sense of weight. Unlike a painting, what we see at the end is what was placed there at the beginning: the polishing simply makes it visible. By carefully applying her chosen materials, rather like a painter with an individual style of brushwork, Catherine has reinvented the art of lacquer.

Nelly Saunier

Plumassière (feather artist)

For more than thirty years, Nelly Saunier has devoted her considerable talents to *plumasserie*, or feather art, combining traditional techniques with individual originality. Stretching back to at least the late 16th century, when the first master *plumassiers* were granted their licences by the French king Henry IV, this ancient craft demands precise knowledge of the material and the techniques that can transform it. These are only learned through a long apprenticeship and working alongside skilled practitioners.

Nelly takes care of every stage of the process – abiding by all the rules and regulations, she buys the feathers, and even sometimes the birds – and her experience and technical prowess (cutting, gluing, etc.) are second to none. However, her biggest challenge of all is to maintain her creative inspiration while fulfilling her clients' wishes. She does this partly by continuing to create original works of her own. Her work is therefore governed by three factors: the creative idea that she executes through her technical expertise, her own creativity that interprets and shapes the project, and the qualities of the material itself.

Working with other outstanding artists, she composes and constructs unique works of art in a kind of symbiosis between creator and material. The work is by its very nature restricted, in the sense that it often depends on ideas proposed by other people or must be adapted to a specific form or context – for example, the face of a clock, the shape of a gemstone or the structure of a hat.

Since embarking on her career, Nelly has collaborated with prestigious names such as Hubert de Givenchy, Nina Ricci, Paco Rabanne, Jean-Charles de Castelbajac and Christian Louboutin. Her collaborations with couturiers have resulted in some of her best-known works, including her parakeet bolero and patterned feather sweater for Jean Paul Gaultier. Today, jewelers and goldsmiths such as Harry Winston present her with a new aesthetic and technical challenge, calling on her to combine feathers and diamonds in their extraordinary creations. Increasingly, however, she has felt the need to make pieces inspired by her own world. She creates purely aesthetic works that play with nature, with the texture and symbolism of the feather as both ornament and protection, and sometimes even with semantics.

Nelly's art gives a second life to birds and, in turn, nature, which is always overflowing with inventiveness and adaptation. She has taught for some twenty years at the Lycée Octave Feuillet, but it is in her workshop that she is best able to pass on her knowledge and her experience to her students.

Alain de Saint-Exupéry

Locksmith

At Château du Fraysse in the Dordogne, the family home that has passed from one generation to the next since the 11th century, Alain de Saint-Exupéry stands in his garden proudly displaying a helicopter that he built himself. His career has been original, to say the least. He came from a family of vine-growers, and his father was cousin to Antoine de Saint-Exupéry, author of *The Little Prince*. He studied mechanical engineering, but found himself more attracted to handicraft and trained to become a cabinetmaker in Paris. Restoring old furniture soon led him to working on locks with lost keys or damaged mechanisms.

When he opened his workshop in 1976, however, the material Alain turned to was wood. 'In marquetry we use wood sawn to a thickness of between 14/10 and 20/10 mm, and I realized that it was becoming difficult to get supplies.' Repairing an old 19th-century saw, he expanded the range of activities offered by his workshop to include the art of sawing and veneering with precious woods. For eighteen years he worked his way round the ateliers in France, delivering his veneers, and the deeper he delved into the mysteries of the arts and crafts, the more tricks of the trade he learned.

Meanwhile, he continued to restore furniture and was increasingly drawn to their locks, which gradually became the main focus of his activity. The opportunity to open an old lock offers a very special experience. Once he has made a key to fit, Alain gains access to the interior of a piece of furniture that may have remained hidden for a hundred years or more. He has restored many genuine masterpieces for museums and collectors, including an exceptional 16th-century chest of forged steel covered with scenes from the life of Hercules.

In 1996, Alain's quest for excellence was recognized when he was asked to join the Grands Ateliers de France, and his perfectionism is only equalled by his desire to pass on his knowledge – to both his son, who also has a gift for mechanical engineering (he specializes in ancient clocks), and the general public. The workshop at the Château du Fraysse is always ready to open its doors to visitors: trainees, antiquarians, curators, private collectors and, on heritage days and the like, anyone who is mildly curious. In 2008, Alain's commitment to the perpetuation of his craft and his sense of community was acknowledged when he was granted the title of *maître d'art*.

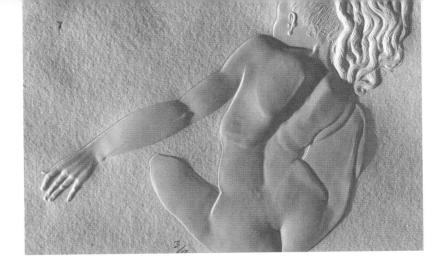

Jean-Luc Seigneur

Engraver and embosser

Seigneur is the French word for 'lord', and in this case, the name could hardly be more appropriate: Jean-Luc is indeed lord of his craft, and teaches engraving at the École Estienne in Paris.

Beginning his career as an engraver, before moving into goffering and hot stamping, Jean-Luc is an artist who uses his skills to pursue his personal ambitions. With his hand-engraved metal dies, he creates luxury embossed bookbindings and upmarket stationery and packaging. He also knows how to adapt to a changing market, offering his services to the finest stationer's in New York, whose clients have included the Duchess of Windsor and Martin Scorsese.

Jean-Luc was quick to realize that his particular talents would only be recognized by an elite audience, and one that would become increasingly demanding, always expecting him to come up with new surprises. As a dedicated artisan, he embraced this challenge and has continued to find new means of self-expression. He sketches nudes and still lifes, which he then turns into relief engravings, enabling them to take on a life of their own. More ambitiously still, he now publishes limited-edition books that he designs and prints himself, sometimes writing the text as well. Parallel to his own artistic career, he also collaborates with artists and designers, introducing them to the traditional techniques of which he is lord and master.

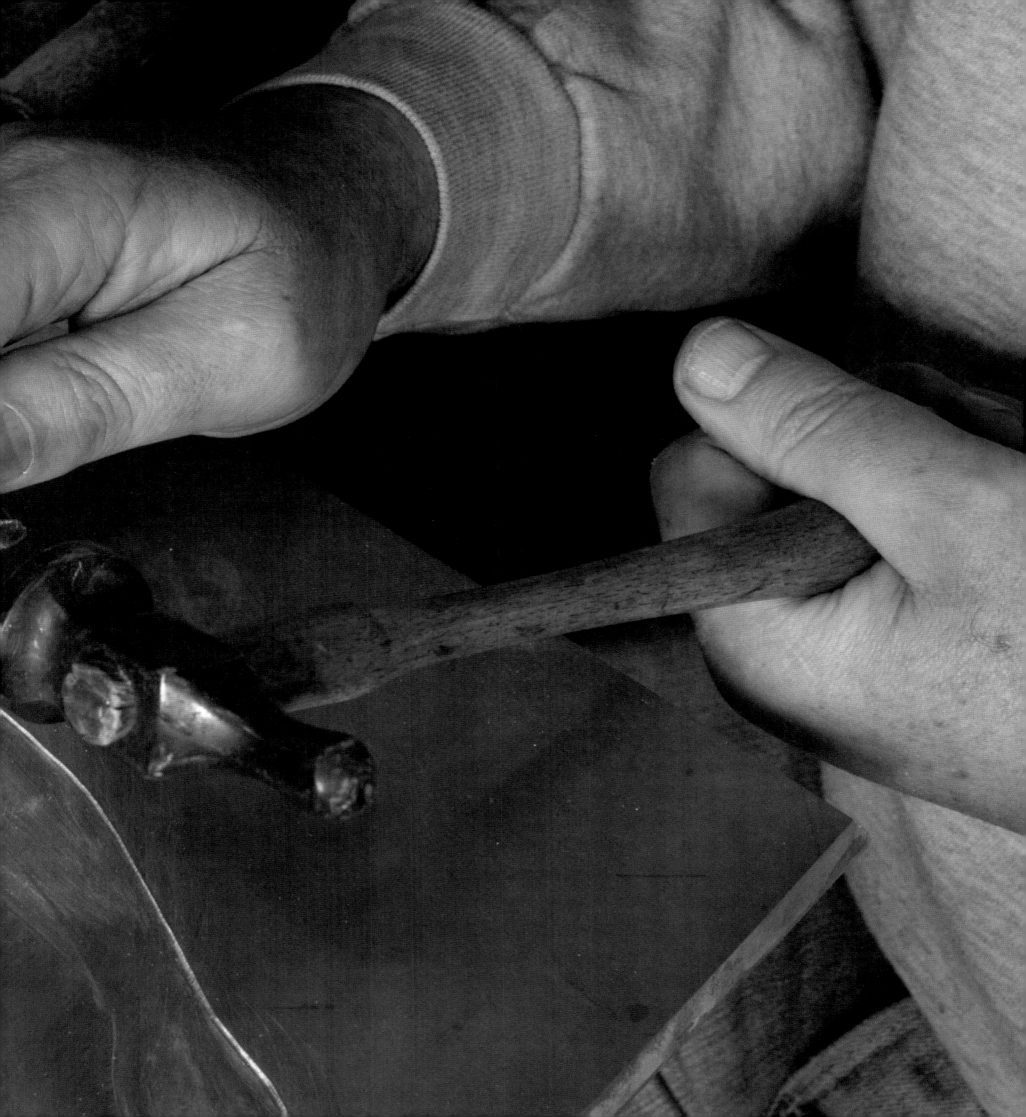

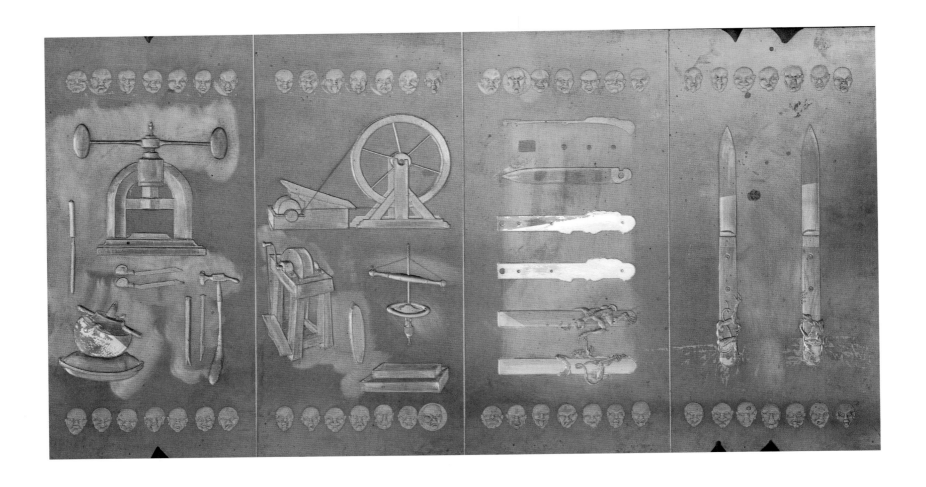

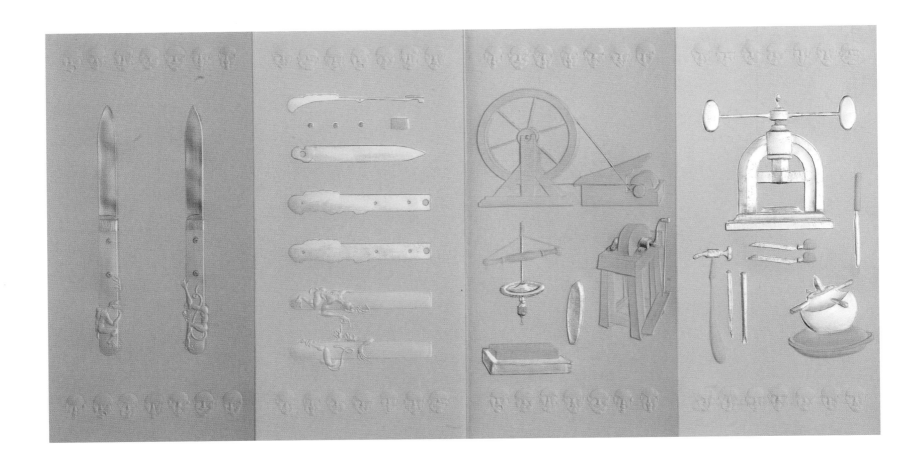

Pietro Seminelli

Textile designer

Pietro Seminelli is a master of the art of fabric folding. This craft did not really exist within the realm of the decorative arts before this remarkable artisan pioneered it, following a great deal of intensive study of both a technical and philosophical nature. Pietro originally trained as a cabinet-maker and interior designer, before entering the worlds of theatre design and haute couture, but it was only after these different experiences that he finally found his own original path.

Just as Pietro was finishing his university studies, Gilles Deleuze published the book *Le pli: Leibniz et le baroque* (1988), which put forward a concept of the fold as a fundamental element within domains as diverse as geology, philosophy, music and the fine arts. Pietro was inspired and embraced the fold as a decorative element, particularly within the realm of textiles. Pleats increase the number of surfaces exposed to light, while different styles of pleat create strength and durability; skilful folding can also create fascinating transparent effects. These striking qualities in Pietro's work have attracted the attention of interior designers such as Peter Marino, Frank de Biasi and Thierry Lemaire, all of whom are bywords for luxury. Pietro's clientele has now expanded to include an increasing number of collectors, galleries and museums such as the Musée des Tissus in Lyons and the Musée des Arts Asiatiques in Nice.

Christian Thirot

ATELIER CHRISTIAN THIROT

Restorer of scientific instruments and glass engraver

As the son of a cabinetmaker, Christian Thirot has been familiar with the workshop environment since he was a child. He was fourteen when he made his first engraving of a squirrel. He went on to spend four years training in a workshop and at the École Estienne in Paris, observing and learning all the tricks of the engraver's trade, and rapidly achieved recognition in his own right.

After finishing his military service, he returned to engraving but decided that mechanical methods were not for him, preferring traditional tools. Two renowned antique dealers gave him the opportunity to resume his work as a copper-plate engraver and master new related skills, including the art of *verre églomisé* (reverse glass gilding) and *sous verre* (painting under glass).

In 1981, he began to devote himself almost exclusively to restoring scientific objects. It was an area of activity that flourished as he learned to work with different materials and a wide variety of rare objects. His clients were mainly collectors and specialist antique dealers.

A successful restoration is one that no one will notice, and Christian has to adapt his methods to suit each individual item in the quest to capture its original character. No matter what the object might be, he must unlock the secrets of the artisans who first constructed it, and he does so with the consummate skill that only comes with many years of experience. His workshop is bursting with complex tools that reflect the precision and discernment that have earned this dedicated artist his reputation.

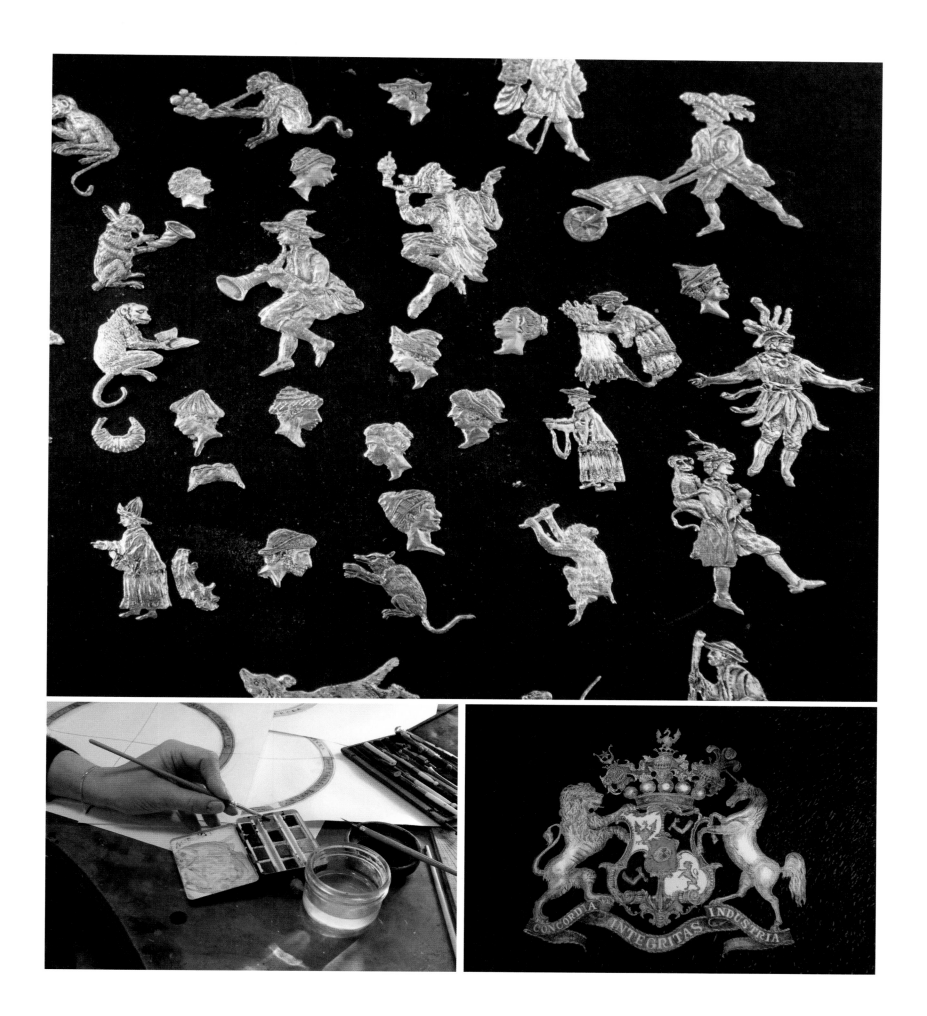

Fanny Boucher
ATELIER HÉLIO'G
Heliographer and intaglio printmaker

Thierry Denis
ATELIERS ASDOURIAN & GUSTAVE GERNEZ
Printmaker and engraver

Stéphane Guilbaud
Lithographer

Guillaume Martel & Manuela Paul-Cavallier
OR DESIGN
Framer and gilder

Étienne de Champfleury
À FLEUR DE PIERRE
Lithographer

Anne-Marie Msili-Jézéquel
Printmaker

Didier Mutel
Engraver and maker of artists' books

Jacky Vignon
Box maker and bookbinder

CHAPTER 5

Art for Art's Sake

Fanny Boucher

ATELIER HÉLIO'G

Heliographer and intaglio printmaker

With a blend of modesty and determination, Fanny Boucher helps artists to translate their ideas into real objects. A visit to an engraving workshop as a girl and trips to the École des Beaux-Arts with an open-minded uncle made a deep impression on her. She later studied at the École Estienne in Paris under Gérard Desquand (see page 162). No matter what task she undertakes – cooperative, creative or educational – she throws herself into it wholeheartedly.

Fanny specializes in heliogravure, a photo-mechanical process that originated in the 19th century and is now practised by only a handful of artists around the world. Heliogravure allows an image to be transferred onto a copper plate by means of photosensitive gelatin, after which it is engraved with acids and then printed manually on an intaglio press. The pH-neutral rag paper on which the heliogravure is printed and the inks made from natural pigments ensure the lasting quality of the prints. Studying under Jean-Daniel Lemoine, a specialist in 19th-century photo-mechanical techniques, Fanny has perfected this craft. Owing to the rarity of this skill,

Hélio'g (founded in 2000) was designated an Entreprise du Patrimoine Vivant (Living Heritage Enterprise) in 2006 and is also on UNESCO's Intangible Cultural Heritage list.

Many well-known figures have entrusted their work to Fanny, from photographers Willy Ronis and Patrick Faigenbaum to artists Pierre Alechinsky, Robert Combas, Zao Wou-Ki, Yayoi Kusama, Tony Soulié, Ernest Pignon-Ernest and François Morellet. The heliogravure process gives works a unique tactile quality, creating an additional sensual dimension. The fine grains of the image create subtle nuances, with deep, dark shades that bear some similarity to velvet.

Fanny has also extended her expertise to interiors and furniture, integrating engraved metal plates into the designs. Revealing the richness of the medium, she creates textures, experiments with light and shade, and uses oxidization effects, often building photographic images into the plates with a technique that is unique to her. She loves the creative process, whether she is working on her own projects or those of other artists.

Thierry Denis

ATELIERS ASDOURIAN & GUSTAVE GERNEZ

Printmaker and engraver

'In the fascinating world of engraved printing, hard work and talent always win out over words,' says Thierry Denis, 'though of course words have their place, everything has its own value, and all we seek is to put tradition to the service of modern life.' As chairman of Ateliers Asdourian & Gustave Gernez, printers and engravers since 1929, he oversees a team of thirty specialists who produce high-quality printed items such as letterheads and cards for a 21st-century clientele.

Using traditional techniques such as copperplate engraving, stamping, embossing and gilding, the team brings out the graphic elements to great effect and turns company stationery and other forms of print into veritable works of art. The team fulfils every commission and ensures that even the humblest notepaper does not leave the premises until it has undergone rigorous inspection. The craftsmanship of their work is striking at a time when printed ephemera is ubiquitous and technology reigns supreme.

Major companies, high-profile figures such as chef Alain Ducasse, luxury Parisian hotels such as the Ritz and the Mandarin Oriental, and state administrative bodies all entrust the workshops with their printed communications. Thierry's success lies in the subtle alchemy that combines a love of beautiful objects, an appreciation of work well done, and a respect for manual skills and techniques passed down through the generations. He finds great satisfaction in opening the eyes of his clients and guiding them towards a choice that is unique both in terms of quality and design.

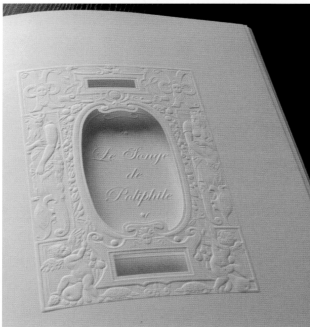

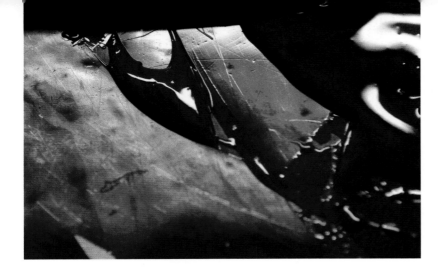

Stéphane Guilbaud

Lithographer

First invented by Alois Senefelder in 1796, lithography is a process of printing from a stone or a metal plate onto which a text or image has been drawn. The flat surface of the stone or plate is treated so that it repels the ink except where it is required for printing. The lithographer, entrusted with the task of transcribing a unique image, could be described as the artist's second right hand and requires a high level of precision in treating the surface of the stone or plate. He or she must also be an exceptional colourist in order to reproduce the precise palette of the painter.

From a young age, Stéphane loved the engravings of Salvador Dalí produced by a friend of his father, and as an amateur he practised lithography in various Parisian workshops as part of his initiation into the fine arts. On the advice of his father's friend, he went to Atelier Desjobert – one of the best workshops for lithography – where he stayed for six years and got to know French painter Olivier Debré. He also went to the Beaux-Arts and the workshop Art Estampe, where he eventually took on the role of director. This was just the beginning of his relationship with a number of famous artists, including Francis Bacon, Balthus, Zao Wou-Ki and Corneille. Stéphane was awarded the title of *maître d'art* in 2010.

Stéphane has two workshops – one in Paris, and the second in the Dordogne – and it is a testament to his skill as a lithographer that artists seek him out. The second workshop is especially suited to the production of large-scale lithographs for it houses a huge Marinoni Voirin flatbed press, built in 1880. This unique machine – the last of its kind in working order – is capable of producing prints up to 120 x 160 cm (47 x 63 in.) in size and was a gift from his colleague Franck Bordas. In the heart of the beautiful French countryside, Stéphane welcomes artists and their families in a cottage near the studio that is entirely at their disposal. Guests have included Gérard Garouste, Yan Pei-Ming, Zhou Chunya and Tony Soulié.

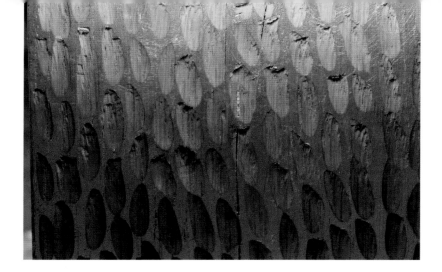

Guillaume Martel & Manuela Paul-Cavallier

OR DESIGN
Framer and gilder

Manuela and Guillaume specialize in gilding and framing respectively – two very different, yet complementary skills. Fascinated by the delicacy and luminosity of gold leaf, Manuela has learned almost all there is to know about gilding techniques. After working in Florence for ten years, she returned to Paris and went from one workshop to another practising her craft. However, it was only when she met Guillaume that she discovered a talent for restoration, which soon brought her to the attention of national museums. Her knowledge encompasses techniques from the 14th to 18th centuries. Through her work with Guillaume, whose rather classical visual and tactile sensibilities were partly inherited from his mother, an antique dealer in Lyons, their shared creative world evolved.

Guillaume loves art, the direct contact with artists and collectors, and the sense of sharing that it brings. It was only natural that he should devote his talents to showing works in the best possible light. In his workshop on the Rue du Regard, a few steps from Montparnasse and the Église Saint-Sulpice, he constructs frames in all shapes and sizes, which Manuela then gilds with painstaking attention to detail and, in particular, colour. Guillaume has a taste for the interplay of light and shade and theatricality in the frames he makes, to which the gold lends itself perfectly. If a frame is bathed in light, it can add substance to the work and even enhance the subject matter of the painting itself.

Since setting up their studio, Or Design, Manuela and Guillaume have worked with interior designers such as Alberto Pinto and Christian Liaigre. Independent of institutions, the studio offers a personalized approach to works that is tailored to the needs of clients and the spaces in which the art is displayed.

Étienne de Champfleury

À FLEUR DE PIERRE
Lithographer

Étienne de Champfleury grew up in a workshop and was familiar with the technique of lithography from an early age. It was his father, Jacques, who founded À Fleur de Pierre in 1974, one of the few remaining workshops to use the traditional method of printing from limestone – a technique that has not changed in more than 200 years. Étienne took over the workshop in 2005 and is determined to pass on the ancient craft, but this does not prevent him from also exploring modern technologies. For instance, he regularly uses the technique of offset lithography, whereby the image is transferred to an intermediate rubber-covered cylinder before being printed.

À Fleur de Pierre, in the heart of the 19th arrondissement in Paris, is autonomous in its use of traditional techniques. It has three hand presses (one French and two German), an enormous machine for large print runs, and an automatic grainer to bring new life to old lithographic stones. The stones that Étienne uses are centuries old, as are the presses of cast iron and wood. Étienne provides all the necessary materials and tools to ensure that works of art are reproduced under optimal conditions, from quantities of brushes and lithographic pencils to large worktables.

At the workshop, he welcomes gallery owners, artists and collectors who appreciate the skill and care he brings to his craft. He enjoys the contacts that he makes through his profession, and takes great pleasure in guiding, supporting and collaborating with creative people, as well as enhancing the value of their work through his own precision and expertise.

Anne-Marie Msili-Jézéquel

Printmaker

When Anne-Marie is asked to reproduce an artist's work, part of her task is to anticipate their wishes and suggest the best way to present their work. She takes a technologically based approach, using an inkjet printer with eleven colours, to which she sometimes adds her own custom-mixed inks to achieve the necessary precision. She also spends a great deal of time at the computer, preparing each piece before creating a print, and then retouching it with coloured pencils in order to produce the desired effect. Most of her prints are done on 100% cotton paper that is specially treated to make the colours stand out.

Anne-Marie studied at the École du Louvre and the École Estienne in Paris. She began with intaglio and lithographic printing, then worked in the field of IT, and returned to printmaking before discovering a way of bringing these two domains together in the early 2000s. Revolutionary new printing processes have now enabled her to combine traditional and contemporary practices. Her collaboration with the great painter Zao Wou-Ki, whose prints also bear the stamp of the atelier, is testament to her skill. When Zao died in 2013, it was to Anne-Marie that the family turned to print their thank-you cards after the funeral.

As well as prints that could be mistaken for originals, she has created wallpaper for the artist Nathalie Talec, art books and photographic prints on linen and cotton, parchment and silk. Most of all, she loves to share her passion for printmaking with her clients, who often become close friends.

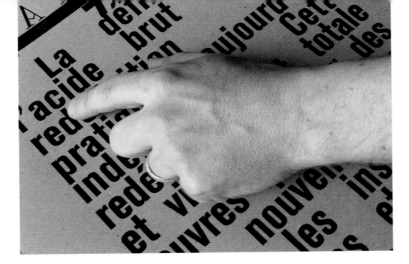

Didier Mutel

Engraver and maker of artists' books

Didier Mutel learned his craft under the expert eye of Pierre Lallier, master engraver at the prestigious Atelier Leblanc in Paris, and it is a connection that he is extremely proud of. Didier's qualifications speak for themselves, with a CV that encompasses the École Estienne, the École Nationale Supérieure des Arts Décoratifs and the Imprimerie Nationale in Paris. However, his forte lies in artists' books, which he shows mainly in France and the US. His works are found in collections around the world, especially in the US, and for two years he was artist in residence at the French Academy's Villa Medici in Rome. Awards include the Grand Prix des Métiers d'Art de la Ville de Paris, the Salon d'Automne prize for artists' books, and the Walter Tiemann Prize in Leipzig.

Didier's grandfather made tools on a workbench that he takes with him wherever he goes, but there is no family history of engraving. Drawing on his natural aptitude, Didier has honed the knowledge passed on to him by Lallier, who was his first tutor and then became his client; he has now worked with him for more than twenty-five years. When Atelier Leblanc closed in 2008, after some 200 years of business, Lallier passed much of its historic material to Didier. After five years of hard work, Didier created his own workshop based on Lallier's teachings and now divides his time between Paris and Orchamps in eastern France, where he hopes to play host to many artists. 'Nowadays I give lectures to American universities about my work,' he says. 'The story of the workshop is symbolic and interests people even beyond our own borders.'

One of the books that Didier has worked on is Robert Louis Stevenson's *The Strange Case of Dr Jekyll and Mr Hyde*, first published in 1886. His own edition, published in 1994, opens with ten etchings that depict a mask of Dr Jekyll transforming into Mr Hyde, but the duality of the Jekyll/Hyde character is also conveyed in the presentation of the text through clever typographical devices: clashing typefaces are used to represent the two characters, with Hyde's large, hollow type gradually dominating as the story progresses; eventually, it becomes so large that the text is rendered illegible. The typography combines ancient and modern techniques, marrying Rembrandt's traditional technique of etching with special computer software, to mirror Jekyll's increasingly disturbed state as he loses control of his metamorphosis.

Didier's books have a low print run of between one and 100 copies and are bought by leading American universities and private collectors. *My Way*, displayed at the Palais de Tokyo in Paris in spring 2013, goes one step further in linking traditional methods with contemporary technology. Attached to the book is a memory stick, which contains a video showing the intaglio work in progress. *My Way* was Didier's first *acide brut* action, in which he explored the effects of acid on a metal plate and of the metal plate on paper. His innovative approach to technique during this project was a kind of joyful, ludic metaphor for decompartmentalization, opening up and redefining the art of engraving.

Jacky Vignon

Box maker and bookbinder

Following an arts-based education and a period spent working as an antique dealer, Jacky Vignon studied bookbinding at the Union des Arts Décoratifs, learning the traditional techniques of leather craft. Bookbinding was the career for which he seemed destined, but this energetic and independently-minded man, with a passion for painting and architecture, swiftly sought to spread his wings beyond the strict confines of the realm of books, although he never lost his deep-rooted attachment to it. A mixture of chance and inspiration led Jacky to the creation of a totally new kind of object: the '*boîtobjetdart*' – a box of decorative leather, and a work of art in itself. It was the perfect outlet for his unconventional and innovative spirit.

Do people store necklaces, rings and other pieces of jewelry in shoeboxes? Of course not! Then nor should they do so with other valuable items or collectables, reasoned Jacky. So it was that he began to create a range of unique and beautiful boxes for all kinds of objects. These boxes are aesthetically very contemporary, and are designed to be exhibited in their own right, as well as serving as a setting for the precious items they hold. For this reason, Jacky is always careful to integrate each box with his client's tastes in decor, allowing them to act as a container within a container. His unique craft combines an understanding of each client's requirements, highly trained technical skills and outstandingly original designs.

Most of his boxes are made to hold objects such as spectacles, watches, gloves or valuable papers, but sometimes Jacky is commissioned to provide a case for something exceptional. The photograph in the bottom right-hand corner of page 332 shows a 'lectern book' commissioned by Japanese clients to commemorate the Fukushima disaster. A violin and bow were made out of wood from trees destroyed by the 2011 earthquake. Violinists from all over the world will be invited to play the violin and then to record their emotions in the handmade book. The book's vellum pages are mounted on guards, and the block formed by the guards encloses a pen case with a magnetic lid. This highly unusual creation is bound entirely in leather and decorated with an image of the last tree left standing by the earthquake.

In addition to making these objets d'art, Jacky also turns his hand to interior decor, devising what he calls 'landscapes of leather' that serve as elegant wall panels and furniture upholstery.

Stéphane Bondu
L'ATELIER DE L'OBJET
Jeweler

Christian Bonnet & Sons
MAISON BONNET
Spectacle makers

Anne-Lise Courchay
Parchment designer

Roland Daraspe
Gold and silversmith

Frédéric Hamel
ÉTABLISSEMENTS FRÉDÉRIC HAMEL
Ivory turner

Nicolas Marischael
Silversmith

Francis & Benoît Migeon
ATELIER MIGEON
Ivory carvers

Ludwig Vogelgesang
ATELIER LUDWIG & DOMINIQUE
Cabinetmaker

CHAPTER 6

Precious Materials

Stéphane Bondu

L'ATELIER DE L'OBJET
Jeweler

Stéphane Bondu is a rare talent, combining an enviable mastery of all the traditional and contemporary techniques of jewelrymaking with a gift for inventing tools and machines. The pieces he creates are so unique that he does not want anyone to see them until they are finished in case they copy them. Every item is a perfect marriage between the original concept and the knowledge of how to transform that idea into a real object.

As a businessman, Stéphane is unassuming but self-assured. From an early age he wanted a career that would involve using his hands, although he ended up studying accountancy. Building on his love of metal, he learned the craft of making boxes, then precious objects, eventually making clocks for Cartier. He founded L'Atelier de l'Objet in 1999.

To make the finest jewels, Stéphane has brought together a number of craftsmen, including enamel workers, *guillocheurs*, setters and engravers – specializations that are increasingly rare. At L'Atelier de l'Objet, everyone still works at a bench, despite having access to all the latest technologies, such as three-dimensional printers and computer software. Here, the precision of the digital world is wedded to the dexterity of the hand. Ultrasonic machines may aid the craftsman in sculpting, turning or engraving the hard stones, but only the human hand can set them in a unique way.

Excellence is at the forefront of the team's work, but they are also driven by a desire to push the boundaries of technique and design. More often than not, as the very best in their own particular fields, they achieve this.

Christian Bonnet & Sons

MAISON BONNET

Spectacle makers

The story of Maison Bonnet dates back to the 1930s, when craftsman Alfred Bonnet – working in Morez, a town known for the manufacture of spectacles – made gold and shell frames his speciality. Maison Bonnet was founded by Alfred's son Robert, and the family's talent for eyewear design and love of this craft passed to his son Christian and his grandson Franck, each of whom has made his own mark on the company. Today, its made-to-measure spectacles are considered among the most prestigious in the world.

Maison Bonnet has specialized in tortoiseshell for decades. Made of keratin, a type of protein that is also found in human skin, hair and nails, tortoiseshell has many qualities: it is light, hypoallergenic, and assumes the temperature of whoever's wearing it, so it does not cause sweat or slip off. The mottled, translucent material comes with many variations of colour, from black and brown to cherry and pink to pure blond.

The Bonnets share a passion for the art of working this material, but perhaps none more so than Christian, who has since been awarded the title of *maître d'art*. He received training from the last two active practitioners in this craft, Jacques Rameau and François Mondon. Since the 1970s, legal restrictions have been in place to protect the species of turtle from which tortoiseshell derives. Maison Bonnet is committed to protecting the species

and sets aside a proportion of the cost of each pair of spectacles for this purpose. Meanwhile, the company works on stocks amassed before the ban.

In recent years, Maison Bonnet has incorporated modern technologies into its designs and expanded its range of materials. It was Christian's son Franck – together with his brother Steven, the youngest member of the family – who propelled the company into the 21st century. Determined to raise his father's profile, Franck found the perfect setting: a magnificent shop-cum-workshop near the Palais Royal in Paris. If you want to create spectacles as unique as a work of art, you need to make yourself visible. It was Steven's idea to make bespoke spectacles in the less expensive buffalo horn as well as in acetate. The company welcomes students recommended by the best schools of optics.

One of the qualities that sets Maison Bonnet apart is its attention to detail. For each custom-made frame, measurements of the upper facial features of the client – nose and the distance between the pupils, for example – are taken. The results speak for themselves, with some customers returning years later to have their beloved spectacles repaired. Taking into consideration the infinite variety of our facial features, Maison Bonnet makes the very idea of standardized spectacle design seem absurd.

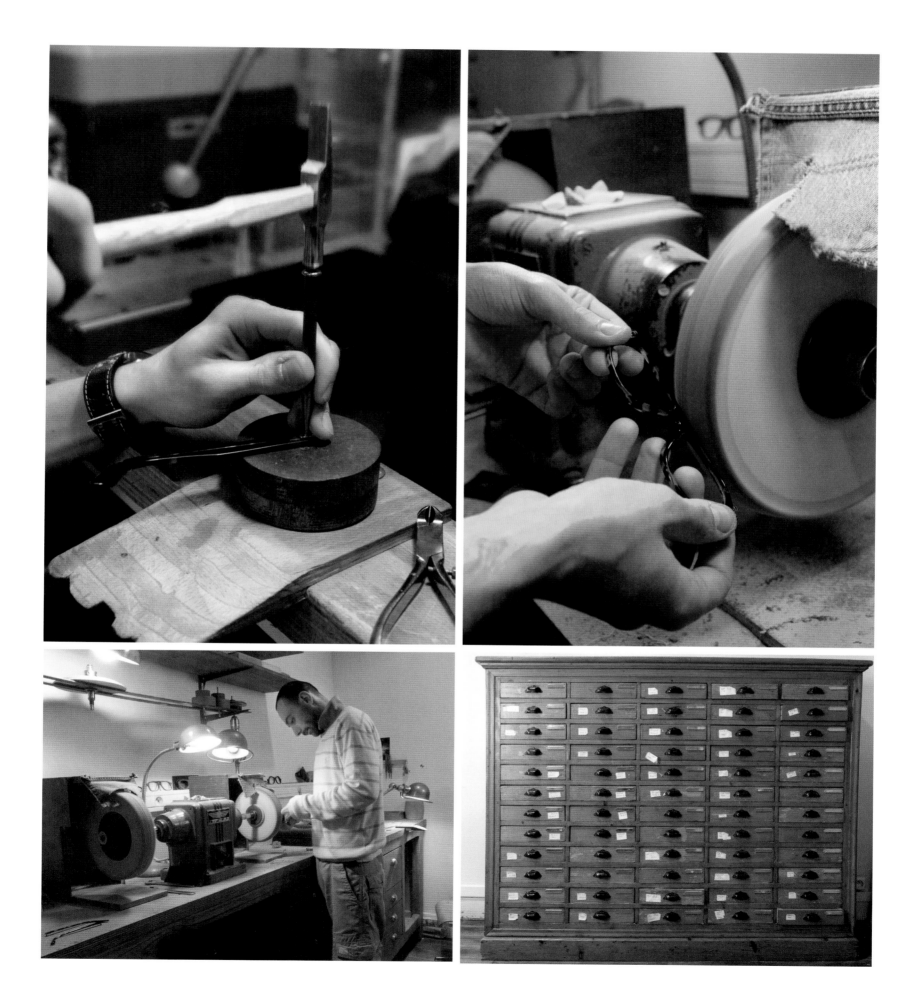

Anne-Lise Courchay

Parchment designer

Anne-Lise Courchay has always had a gift for drawing and painting. After studying history of art, architecture and bookbinding, she set out to gain professional experience. With her discovery of parchment, a thin material made from animal hide, her plans were turned on their head. On studying these creamy white, traditionally smooth skins, Anne-Lise hit on the idea of preserving their natural colours by modifying the process of fabrication. Just like a painter, she set to work enhancing the texture that gives the skins their character. In her parchments, the focus lies on the traces of hair and the ochry, earthy, greyish hues that make them unique.

Anne-Lise is based in Montreuil, in the eastern suburbs of Paris, where her beautiful, airy workshop gives her all the space she needs to expand her repertoire. The pieces presented in these pages are just a small sample of her work. She buys the skins in a natural state, and is particularly fond of goatskin, which is exceptionally fine and has a very special texture. The equipment in her workshop enables her to work these skins in a thousand different ways – pressing them, dyeing them, and sometimes even stretching them until they are almost transparent. At this point, she begins to design her parchment.

Her efforts in realizing the enormous potential of parchment were acknowledged in 2003 when she was awarded the Liliane Bettencourt Prize for Handicraft. Her mission, which she pursues with unabated determination, is to raise the status of parchment by every technical means possible, in domains as varied as bookbinding, interior design and haute couture. She has even invented a term to describe her profession: 'parchment designer'.

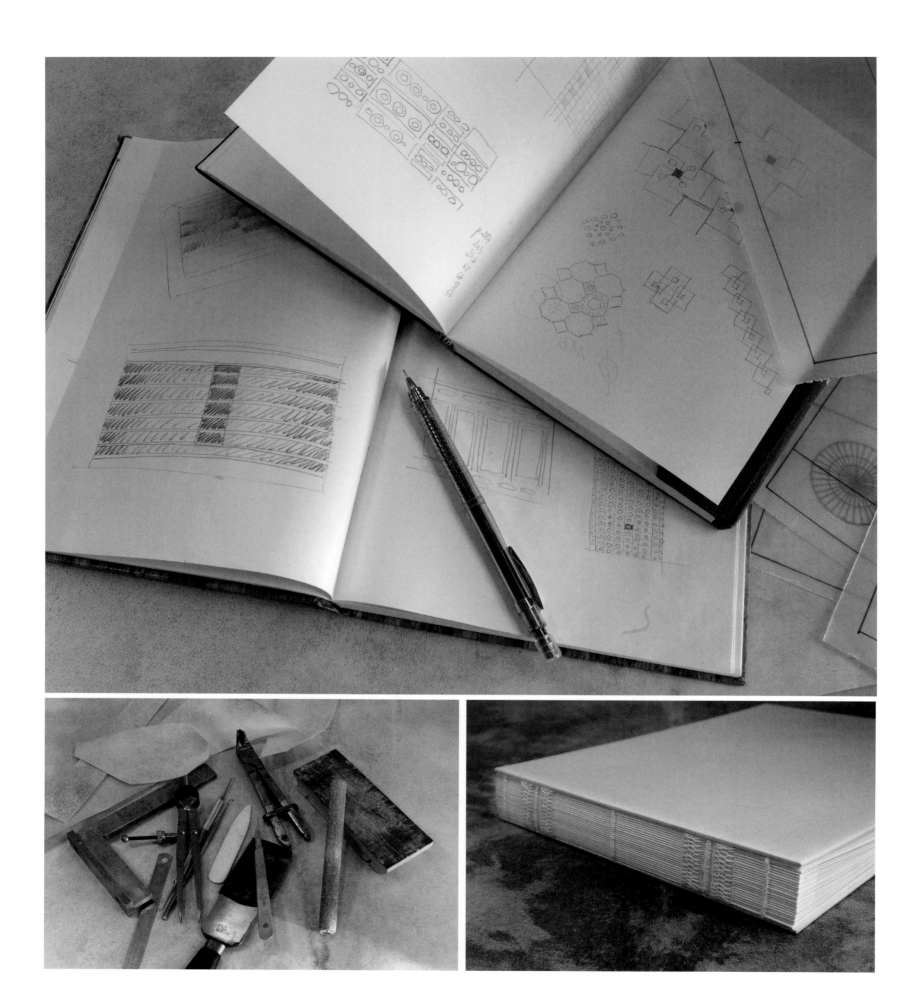

Roland Daraspe

Gold and silversmith

Based in the Bordeaux region of France, Roland Daraspe began his career as a coppersmith and aeronautical engineer but turned to making jewelry in 1975. His life has centred around his creative work ever since, and he was awarded the title of *maître d'art* in 2002. His favourite metal is silver, which demands all the energy and attention of the craftsman who shapes it – an art that Roland learned all on his own. Even when he uses brass, for example in his architectural projects, he approaches it in the tradition of the great silversmiths.

In 1992, Jacqueline du Pasquier, curator at the Musée des Arts Décoratifs de Bordeaux, presented a retrospective of Roland's work. This not only gave him a wonderful boost personally, but also led to increasingly complex commissions, which sharpened his imagination and took him into new areas. In 2008, the same museum, under the direction of Bernadette de Boysson, and the Musée des Beaux Arts in Carcassonne mounted an exhibition of his later works. Roland's achievements have won him recognition in the world of contemporary art, cemented by his numerous awards and appointment to the Académie Nationale des Sciences, Belles-Lettres et Arts de Bordeaux. His style – a balance between organic subtlety and daring originality – is unmistakably his own.

The work of a silversmith goes through several phases: imagination, sketches, drawings, models, hard work, deafening blows of the hammer, and endless devotion to the precious though ever-demanding metal from which the object eventually takes form. Roland loves a challenge that takes him beyond the repetitive aspects of his craft. Time and experience have given him an inner strength and unshakeable confidence because he knows that in due course the magical transformation will always take place and bring him a kind of euphoria. In order to master the material, Roland must read its mind, engage it in battle, and with hand and with fire emerge the victor. He is always happy when a piece is complete, with a perfect finish, functional, durable, and beautiful to see and touch. That is how silver work should always be – a precious material made still more precious by the man who has mastered it.

Frédéric Hamel

ÉTABLISSEMENTS FRÉDÉRIC HAMEL
Ivory turner

Only a handful of artisans have mastered the technique of ivory turning. Frédéric Hamel learned this craft at the École Boulle and perfected it at the Atelier Pierre Meyer, under the tutelage of the master craftsman himself. Complying with the strict regulations that govern the use of ivory, he makes guilloche mouldings for frames, boxes, decorative objects and auctioneers' hammers; he also makes pommels for walking sticks, although in recent years these have often been made from synthetic ivory or exotic wood.

Frédéric works in Neuilly-sur-Marne, in the eastern suburbs of Paris, with his partner Bilana Jovic, an engraver who also studied at the École Boulle. Both are skilled in a range of techniques and materials, from precious woods, stone and bone to mother-of-pearl and horn. In addition to turning ivory, Frédéric also excels in marquetry, inlay, lapidary work, milling, linear guilloche, restoration and engraving. This versatility has enabled him to practise his profession while at the same time widening his circle of contacts and ensuring his autonomy.

In 2007, his workshop was awarded Living Heritage Enterprise status, which earned him wider recognition of his expertise; this distinction was renewed in 2013. His imagination and ability to work with different techniques have won him a prestigious clientele, including luxury brands, artisans in other fields, creative artists and art dealers.

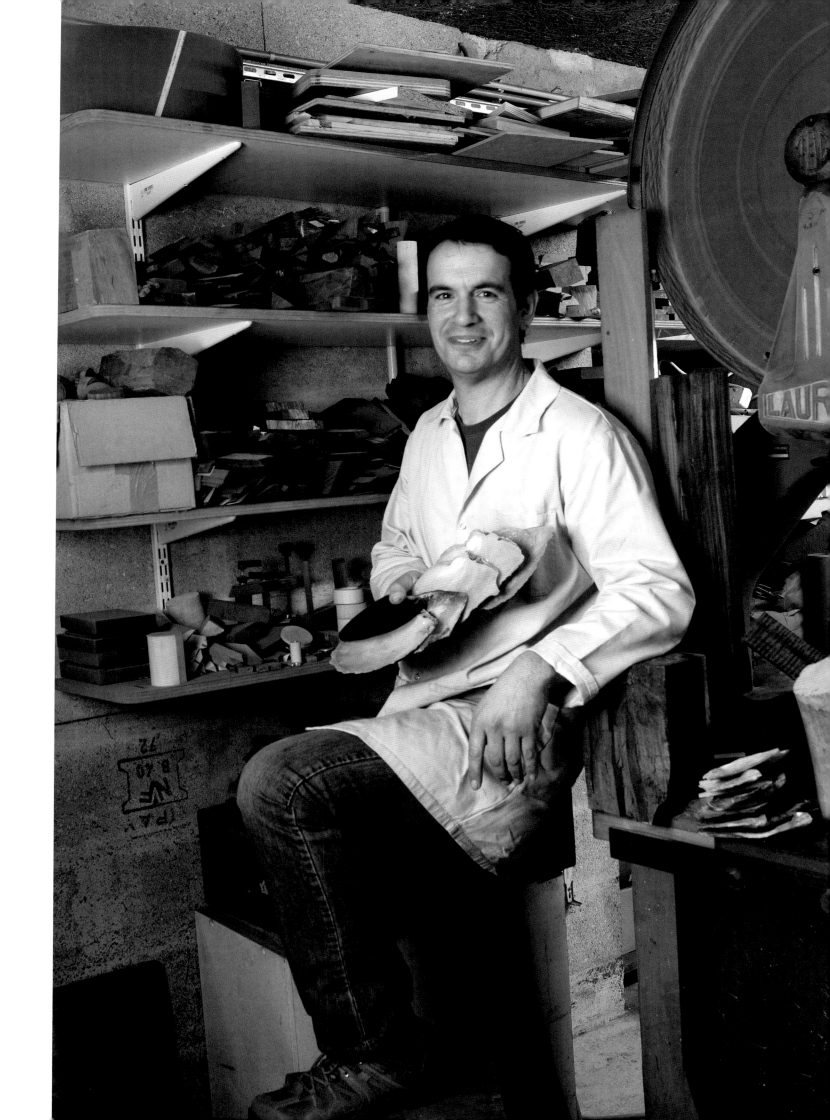

Nicolas Marischael

Silversmith

Whether he is restoring works from the 18th century or turning his hand to his own creations, Nicolas displays a rare mastery of silver. It is a talent that goes back several generations: both his father and his grandfather were gifted silversmiths. For years the Marischaels worked in the Marais quarter of Paris, but today the workshop is in the modern, prestigious Viaduc des Arts, where his clientele includes private collectors, dealers and museums. The atmosphere – a blend of the traditional and the modern – is ideal for Nicolas's art.

In order to practise his craft at the highest level, Nicolas demonstrates his persistence and discipline – the same qualities that won him a place in the national water polo team when he was a boy, and the chance to compete in the Seoul Olympic Games in 1988. As a member of the Grands Ateliers de France, he is master of all facets of the silversmith's craft, including forging, planishing and chasing. As well as restoring antique items, he designs and makes his own pieces and today ranks as one of the leading lights of contemporary silverware.

The versatile Nicolas is constantly coming up with new and inventive approaches to silver work, yet at the same time he is refreshingly modest. He is widely recognized for the originality and high quality of his work, and in 2011 his workshop was given Living Heritage Enterprise status, a distinction awarded by the French Ministry of Economy, Finance and Industry to reward firms for their excellence in traditional and industrial skills.

Francis & Benoît Migeon

ATELIER MIGEON

Ivory carvers

'I defend my craft by saying that the work is not forbidden but regulated!' declares Francis, an octogenarian still actively engaged in carving ivory. He works on the stocks he acquired before the introduction of laws banning the unregulated sale of ivory – a move that, incidentally, he approves of. The new laws put in place to protect the elephant allow the trade of antique worked specimens of ivory acquired in their finished state before 1947 when accompanied by the appropriate certification. Despite these laws governing domestic and international trade, the tusks of elephants hunted during colonial rule continue to appear on the market.

Francis developed his love of the art from his father Amédée and never wanted to do anything else. In fact, the Migeon family, fathers and sons, have been ivory carvers for four generations. Célestin paved the way in 1895, producing 'great religious ivories'. His son Adrien was active in the Art Deco period: one of his statuettes is on show at the Musée de la Céramique et de l'Ivoire in Commercy. Now it is Francis's son, Benoît, who is taking on the mantle: after attending the École Boulle in Paris, where he was initially drawn to cabinetmaking, he joined his father's workshop; these days he has his own workshop and lives in Brittany. Each generation has inherited this passion for a material that is as hard as it is fragile, and that reveals the most extraordinary patterns when it is polished. 'The colour is unique, and the texture fascinating,' says Francis.

Benoît brings out all the qualities of this material. With his files and chisels, he polishes and refines the shapes and, like a contemporary sculptor, recycles every cubic centimetre. Nowadays, boxes, missals and religious items, sewing cases and other decorative items can only be restored, but the shavings are used for objects to delight ivory lovers.

Ludwig Vogelgesang

ATELIER LUDWIG & DOMINIQUE
Cabinetmaker

'One must caress the forms,' says Ludwig, who is originally from Germany. It is a fitting description for the work of a multi-talented man whose love of materials undoubtedly played a part in his decision to become a furniture restorer. Choosing Paris as his base, he was able to learn his craft from a master with expertise in the 18th century. Having been seduced by the Art Deco style, he specializes in rare pieces of furniture from the early 20th century for a prestigious clientele that includes museums and auction houses.

The workshop was established in 1980 as a joint enterprise with Dominique, who has since retired, and still operates under the name Ludwig & Dominique. It comprises a team of people who not only work together but also enjoy one another's company and are constantly exchanging ideas about forms, materials and the history of every object that comes their way. The team has been joined by Marina, who has brought an outsider's view of their craft; her presence has become integral to their success, thanks to her artistic instinct, her realistic approach, and her lively but critical mind. In association with a wide network of reliable artisans – carpet makers, upholsterers, ironworkers, mirror makers, polishers, inlayers, marblers,

engravers, bronzesmiths, gilders and others from the Grands Ateliers de France – Ludwig & Dominique can take on the complete restoration of an item of furniture and has justifiably won praise for its contribution to French heritage.

Ludwig has been awarded the title of *maître d'art* in recognition of the outstanding quality of his restorations and original work. One of his favourite materials is shagreen, or shark skin. This precious and delicate material is very time-consuming and difficult to work, but Ludwig and his team of qualified cabinetmakers have the necessary skills to meet the challenge and achieve the best possible results. Mother-of-pearl, mica, straw, parchment and precious woods are all handled with complete mastery of traditional methods such as French polishing, as well as vacuum metallizing and other modern techniques.

The workshop acts as a veritable research consultancy due to the combined knowledge of this team. They can create virtually any rare item, even if the starting point is nothing but an idea or a simple sketch. That does not make them complacent – no one is perfect – but in Ludwig's workshop it is certainly true to say they explore, innovate and continually try to improve.

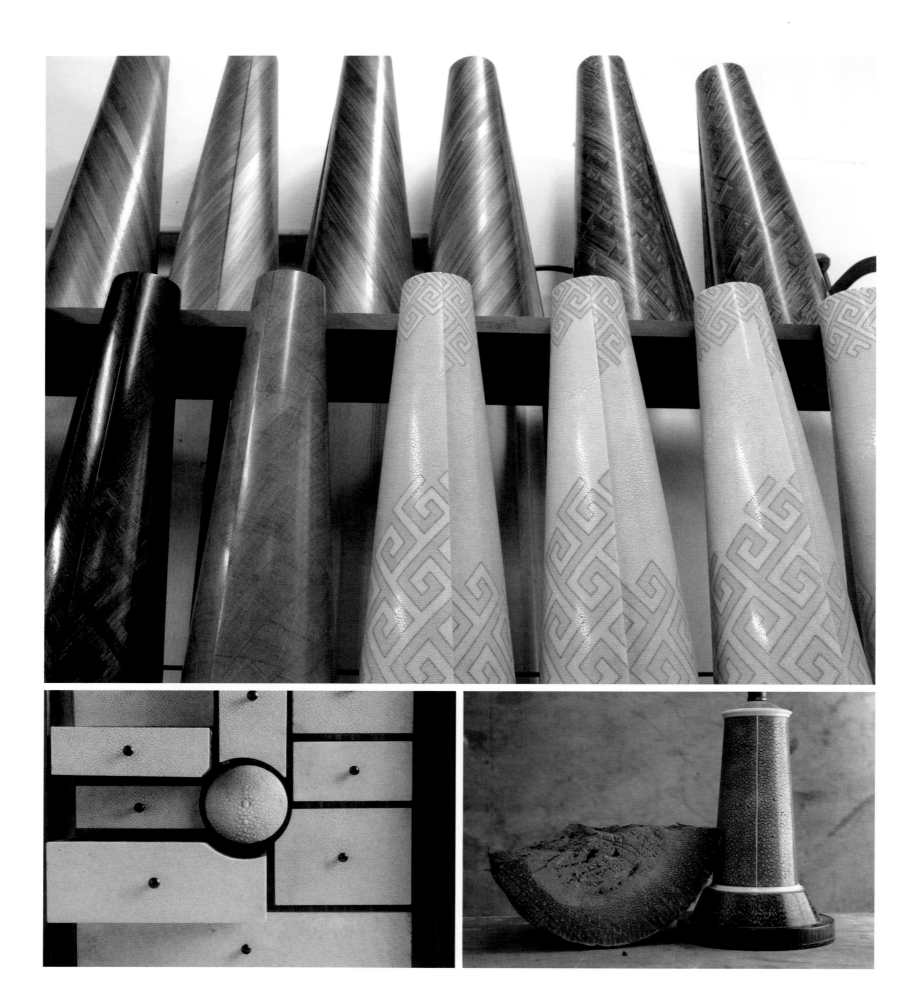

List of Addresses

Grands Ateliers de France
Executive Officer: Stéfan Geissler
Tel: + 33 (0)6 11 71 45 37
contact@grandsateliersdefrance.com
www.grandsateliersdefrance.com

Serge Amoruso Design
13 rue Abel
75012 Paris
Tel: + 33 (0)1 43 45 14 10
Fax: + 33 (0)1 43 40 83 66
Email: serge.amoruso@live.fr

Art & Ors
Represented by Youri Dmitrenko
2 bis rue Dupont de l'Eure
75020 Paris
Tel/Fax: + 33 (0)1 40 30 40 83
Email: art.ors@orange.fr

Atelier Artis – Groupe Villemain
Thomas Vieweger &
Aude Vieweger de Cordoüe
65 avenue de Saumur - Etables
86170 Blaslay
Tel: + 33 (0)5 49 54 42 47
Fax: + 33 (0)5 49 39 40 72
Email: atelier.artis@groupe-villemain.eu

Ateliers Asdourian & Gustave Gernez
Represented by Thierry Denis
60 rue Louveau
92320 Châtillon
Tel: + 33 (0)1 47 35 81 01
Fax: + 33 (0)1 47 35 20 67
Email: t.denis@asdouriangernez.com
www.asdouriangernez.com

Le Bégonia d'Or
Sylvie Deschamps
67 avenue Charles de Gaulle
17300 Rochefort
Tel: + 33 (0)5 46 87 59 36
Fax: + 33 (0)5 46 87 59 37
Email: begonia-d-or@wanadoo.fr

Atelier Patrick Blanchard
199 avenue de la Division Leclerc
95880 Enghien-les-Bains
Tel/Fax: + 33 (0)1 39 64 13 52
Email: blanchardsculpt@hotmail.fr

Élise Blouet-Ménard
Tel: + 33 (6) 79 97 95 44
Email: eblouet@hotmail.com
www.eliseblouet.com

Stéphane Bondu
L'Atelier de l'Objet
6 rue du Mont-Thabor
75001 Paris
Tel: + 33 (0)1 42 97 54 67
Fax: + 33 (0)1 42 97 53 72
Email: atelier.objet@laposte.net

Atelier Pierre Bonnefille
Showroom: 5 rue Bréguet
75011 Paris
Tel: + 33 (0)1 43 55 06 84

Fax: + 33 (0)1 43 55 04 92
Email: contact@pierrebonnefille.com
www.pierrebonnefille.com

Maison Bonnet
Atelier: 3 bis rue de la Cordellerie
89100 Sens
Boutique: 5 passage des Deux Pavillons
5 rue des Petits Champs
75001 Paris
Tel: + 33 (0)3 86 95 22 70
Fax: + 33 (0)3 86 65 40 88
Email: contact@maisonbonnet.com
www.maisonbonnet.com

Atelier Alain Bouchardon
10 avenue Foch
60300 Senlis
Tel: + 33 (0)3 44 53 10 15
Fax: + 33 (0)3 44 53 39 73
Email: atelierbouchardon@orange.fr

Fanny Boucher
Hélio'g
Atelier no. 12
Potager du Dauphin
15 rue Porto-Riche
92190 Meudon
Tel/Fax: + 33 (0)1 46 44 65 12
Email: fanny@heliog.com
www.heliog.com

Maison Brazet
Represented by Rémy Brazet
22 rue des Belles-Feuilles
75116 Paris
Tel: + 33 (0)1 47 27 20 89
Fax: + 33 (0)1 47 55 68 90
Email: maisonbrazet@wanadoo.fr
www.maisonbrazet.fr

Christian Broggini
La Maison Lumière
30 rue Nollet
75017 Paris
Tel: + 33 (0)9 54 19 30 30
Email: broggini.christian@gmail.com

Hervé Bruchet
Atelier Darne – Fort Royal
Represented by Jacques Bolelli
32 boulevard de la Bastille
75012 Paris
Tel: + 33 (0)1 83 64 89 12
Email: contact@fort-royal.com
www.fort-royal.com

Atelier Lison de Caunes
20 rue Mayet
75006 Paris
Tel: + 33 (0)1 40 56 02 10
Fax: + 33 (0)1 42 19 93 70
Email: lison.decaunes@free.fr
www.lisondecaunes.com

Gilles Chabrier
36 boulevard de la Bastille
75012 Paris
Tel: + 33 (0)1 43 43 36 00

Fax: + 33 (0)1 43 43 17 65
Email: contact@gilleschabrier.com
www.gilleschabrier.com

Étienne de Champfleury
À Fleur de Pierre
17 rue de Nantes
75019 Paris
Tel: + 33 (0)1 40 36 52 52
Fax: + 33 (0)1 40 36 53 56
Email: artlitho@club-internet.fr

Caroline Corrigan
18 avenue Foch
93360 Neuilly-Plaisance
Tel: + 33 (0)1 43 81 94 47
Email: caroline.corrigan@wanadoo.fr

Corthay Bottier
Represented by Pierre Corthay
Boutique-atelier: 1 rue Volney
75002 Paris
Tel: + 33 (0)1 42 61 08 89
Fax: + 33 (0)1 42 61 04 00
Email: contact@corthay.com
www.corthay.fr

Anne-Lise Courchay
Atelier no. 7
13 rue Henri Schmitt
93100 Montreuil
Tel: + 33 (0)1 48 57 21 10 / + 33 (0)6 73 03 80 70
Email: annelise.courchay@sfr.fr
www.livre-luxe-parchemin.com

Roland Daraspe
6 chemin du Tayet
33460 Macau
Tel: + 33 (0)5 57 88 48 79
Email: daraspe@daraspe.com
www.daraspe.com

Gérard Desquand
7 rue Oberkampf
75011 Paris
Tel/Fax: + 33 (0)1 43 38 33 21
Email: gerard@desquand.fr
www.desquand.fr

Atelier Drevelle
Represented by Christian-Thierry Drevelle
134 rue de la République
16100 Cognac
Tel: + 33 (0)5 45 32 09 97
Fax: + 33 (0)5 45 36 51 40
Email: ctdrevelle@drevelle.com
www.drevelle.com

Marie Dubost
L'Atelier de la Feuille d'Or
173 rue du Faubourg Saint Antoine
75011 Paris
Tel/Fax: + 33 (0)1 40 02 02 65
Email: m.dubost@cegetel.net

Dunod-Mallier
Represented by Mehdi Mallier
28 avenue des Trois Peuples
78180 Montigny-le-Bretonneux

Tel: + 33 (0)1 30 47 15 31
Fax: + 33 (0)1 30 47 21 06
Email: mehdi@dunodmallier.fr
www.dunodmallier.fr

Atelier Simon-Pierre Étienne
20 rue Bouvier
75011 Paris
Tel: + 33 (0)1 43 72 33 39
Fax: + 33 (0)1 43 72 33 50
Email: spe3@wanadoo.fr

Atelier Sébastien Evain
53 rue Brancion
75015 Paris
Tel: + 33 (0)1 48 56 20 12
Email: evain-sebastien@gmail.com

Patrick Fallon
337 route de Valparc
74330 Poissy / Annecy
Tel: + 33 (0)4 50 24 01 44
Fax: + 33 (0)4 50 24 00 43
Email: fallon@wanadoo.fr
www.falloncuir.com

Atelier Caroline & Tristan Fournier
1 rue de Verdonnet
63910 Bouzel
Tel/Fax: + 33 (0)4 73 68 19 93
Email: tristanfournier.models@gmail.com
www.art-auto-de-luxe-c-t-fournier.fr

Yves Gaignet
10 rue Jacquemont
75017 Paris
Tel: + 33 (0)6 14 09 39 05 / + 33 (0)1 58 60 17 51
Email: shipshapes-models@wanadoo.fr
www.shipshapes-models.com

Michel Germond
63 rue de Vaugirard
75006 Paris
Tel: + 33 (0)6 08 24 46 56
Email: m.j.germond@wanadoo.fr

Stéphane Guilbaud
Tel: + 33 (0)6 08 90 37 31
Email: contact@artslitho.com
www.atelierstephaneguilbaud.com

Établissements Frédéric Hamel
80 bis rue du 11 Novembre
93330 Neuilly sur Marne
Tel/Fax: + 33 (0)1 43 08 90 41
Email: etshamel@wanadoo.fr

Atelier Edgard Hamon
Represented by Dragui Romic & Arnaud Paix
5 rue d'Uzès
75002 Paris
Tel: + 33 (0)1 44 82 84 40
Email: veroniquelamotte@edgardhamon.fr
www.edgardhamon.com

Mireille Herbst
ALM Déco
10 rue André Joineau
93310 Le Pré Saint Gervais

Tel: + 33 (0)1 48 91 98 64
Fax: + 33 (0)1 48 91 02 71
Email: alm.deco@free.fr

Michel Heurtault
Parasolerie Heurtault
85 avenue Daumesnil
75012 Paris
Tel: + 33 (0)1 44 73 45 71
Email: parasolerie.heurtault@gmail.com
www.parasolerieheurtault.com

Françoise Hoffmann
5 rue Bodin
69001 Lyons
Tel: + 33 (0)4 26 00 28 23
Email: francoise.hoffmann@club-internet.fr
www.francoisehoffmann.com

Robert Jallet
5 rue de Charonne
75011 Paris
Tel/Fax: + 33 (0)1 47 00 26 64
Email: jal_sieges@wanadoo.fr

Marie Le Cœur
34 boulevard Saint-Jacques
75014 Paris
Tel/Fax: + 33 (0)1 45 35 49 38
Email: lecoeur.marie@neuf.fr

Gwénola Le Masson
Atelier l'Amarante
171 rue du Faubourg Saint Antoine
75011 Paris
Tel/Fax: + 33 (0)1 49 28 00 38
Email: atelieramarante@wanadoo.fr

Lemerle Frères
62 rue Legendre
75017 Paris
Tel: + 33 (0)1 46 22 28 56
Email: lemerlefreres@wanadoo.fr
http://gainier-lemerle.com

Fanny Liautard
13 rue Saint-Florentin
75008 Paris
Tel: + 33 (0)1 42 86 82 84
Email: fanny@fannyliautard.com
www.fannyliautard.com

Ludwig & Dominique
Represented by Ludwig Vogelgesang
2 ter passage Ramey
75018 Paris
Tel: + 33 (0)1 42 59 81 15
Fax: + 33 (0)1 42 59 81 30
Email: dolu@club-internet.fr
www.ebeniste-art-deco-paris.fr

Rachida Mallogi
Ame de Laine et de Soie
18 chemin du Moulin à Vent
13940 Molleges
Tel: + 33 (0)4 90 95 07 03
Email: mallogi.rachida@wanadoo.fr
www.rachidamallogi.fr

Atelier Maonia
Represented by Marine Fouquet
& Hervé Morin
8 passage Brulon
75012 Paris
Tel: + 33 (0)9 51 51 03 26
Email: maonia@free.fr

Nicolas Marischael
87 avenue Daumesnil
75012 Paris
Tel: + 33 (0)1 42 78 07 63
Fax: + 33 (0)1 42 78 53 67
Email: nicolas@marischael.com
www.marischael.com

Atelier Simon Marq – Fort Royal
Represented by Jacques Bolelli
44 rue Ponsardin
51100 Reims
Tel: + 33 (0)3 26 47 23 15
Email: j.bolelli@fort-royal.com
Paris address: Fort Royal
32 boulevard de la Bastille
75012 Paris
Tel: + 33 (0)1 83 64 89 12
www.atelier-simon-marq.fr
www.fort-royal.com

Guillaume Martel & Manuela Paul-Cavallier
Or Design
2 rue du Regard
75006 Paris
Tel/Fax: + 33 (0)1 45 49 02 07
Email: contact@or-design.fr
www.or-design.fr

Atelier Migeon
Francis Migeon
5 avenue de la Trémouille
94100 Saint-Maur
Tel: + 33 (0)1 42 83 85 88
Fax: + 33 (0) 42 83 58 48
Email: francis.migeon@orange.fr
Benoît Migeon
'Trénéluës', 56660 Saint-Jean Brévelay
Tel/Fax: + 33 (0)2 97 60 47 83
Email: atelierbmigeon@orange.fr

Fernando Moreira
78 quai de l'Hôtel de Ville
75004 Paris
Tel: + 33 (0)1 43 72 91 72
Email: ateliermoreira@wanadoo.fr

Anne-Marie Msili-Jézéquel
1 rue Biscornet
75012 Paris
Tel: + 33 (0)9 81 23 01 10
Email: a2mj@similart.net

Didier Mutel
184 rue de Crimée
75018 Paris
Tel: + 33 (0)1 40 35 06 80
Email: mutel.didier@neuf.fr
atelierdidiermutel.com / didiermutel.com

Atelier von Nagel
Represented by Reinhard von Nagel
20 rue Bouvier
75011 Paris
Tel: + 33 (0)1 44 93 20 93
Fax: + 33 (0)1 44 93 20 94
Email: vonnagel@sfr.fr
www.vonnagel.com

Catherine Nicolas
35 rue du 8 mai 1945
94700 Maisons-Alfort
Tel: + 33 (0)1 43 68 62 61
Email: nicolascath@wanadoo.fr

Anne Nicolle
Atelier Renouvel
3 rue Elzévir
75003 Paris
Tel: + 33 (0)1 42 72 15 28

Thomas Niemann
283 avenue du Président Roosevelt
45220 Château-Renard
Tel: + 33 (0)2 38 28 54 71
Email: melinda.noulin@orange.fr

Laurent Nogues
Créanog
Viaduc des Arts
9 avenue Daumesnil
75012 Paris
Tel: + 33 (0)1 55 78 82 80
Email: laurent.nogues@creanog.com

Ateliers Bernard Pictet
47 rue Oberkampf
75011 Paris
Tel: + 33 (0)1 48 06 19 25
Fax: + 33 (0)1 43 55 31 45
Email: ateliers@bernardpictet.com
www.bernardpictet.com

Atelier Steaven Richard
27 rue de la Folie-Méricourt
75011 Paris
Tel: +33 (0)1 43 38 58 71
Email: atelier@steavenrichard.fr
www.steavenrichard.fr

Alain de Saint-Exupéry
Château du Fraysse
24120 Terrasson
Tel/Fax: + 33 (0)5 53 50 00 05
Email: lefraysse@sfr.fr

Atelier Nicolas Salagnac
3 rue de la Quarantaine
69005 Lyons
Atelier: 45/47 rue Alexis Perroncel
69100 Villeurbanne
Tel: + 33 (0)9 50 32 62 45
Email: contact@nicolas-salagnac.com
www.nicolas-salagnac.com

Nelly Saunier
47 boulevard Saint-Jacques
75014 Paris
Tel: + 33 (0)6 60 95 67 31
Email: nellysaunier@yahoo.fr

Jean-Luc Seigneur
5 allée Charlotte
93360 Neuilly-Plaisance
Tel: + 33 (0)1 43 00 58 03
Email: jeanlucseigneur@wanadoo.fr
www.jeanluc-seigneur.com

Pietro Seminelli
Sté Artésina
Le Neufbourg
Lieu dit 'Le Loup Pendu'
14330 Le Molay Littry
Tel: + 33 (0)2 31 51 92 79
Fax: + 33 (0)2 72 68 56 30
Email: pietro@seminelli.com
www.seminelli.com

Atelier Christian Thirot
26 rue René et Pierre Charton
93250 Villemomble
Tel/Fax: + 33 (0)1 48 54 57 69
Email: christian.thirot@orange.fr

Verrier Père & Fils
Represented by Yves Dorget
10 rue Orfila
75020 Paris
Tel: + 33 (0)1 46 36 49 01
Fax: + 33 (0)1 46 36 83 41
Email: yves.dorget@passementerie-verrier.com
www.passementerie-verrier.com

Jacky Vignon
2 rue Gonnet
75011 Paris
Tel/Fax: + 33 (0)1 44 64 78 28
Email: vignon.jacky@wanadoo.fr
www.jackyvignon.fr

Michel Germond

Pierre Bonnefille

Pierre Bonnefille in his atelier.

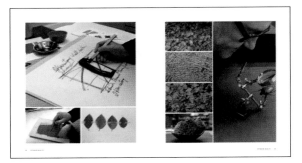

Christian Broggini

The Bordeauxthèque at the Galeries Lafayette department store, Paris, with lighting designed by the Maison Lumière.

Lison de Caunes

Lison in her atelier, working on the restoration of a 19th-century box. On the left is the *Bamboo* screen, designed in 2005 for an exhibition in Beijing.

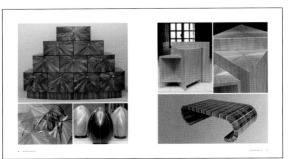

p. 28, above: Pyramid chest of drawers, in green straw marquetry with violet fillets. p. 29, above: Set of nesting tables, reissued by Hermès from a design by Jean-Michel Frank. Below: *Madras* table, 2010.

p. 30: Restoration of a 'prisoner of war' box for the Musée de La Seyne-sur-Mer. Straw marquetry was often practised by prisoners during the Napoleonic wars. p. 31: Some of the 18th- and 19th-century objects from Lison's collection.

Marine Fouquet & Hervé Morin

p. 34, above: *Aléa* screen in dyed straw marquetry with mother-of-pearl fillets and base.

Mireille Herbst

p. 38: Table base, believed to be the *Yucca* design by René Lalique.
p. 39: Detail of *Monkeys* screen by Paul-Étienne Saïn, designed in 1930.

Xavier, Johann & Bruno Lemerle

p. 44, above, and p. 45: Some of the atelier's large collection of finishing tools. p. 44, below: Dyed leather, ready to be used to upholster chairs. Johann works the dyed leather by hand to soften it and enhance its grain.

Marie Le Cœur

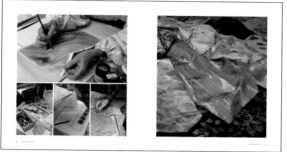

Fabric requires careful preparation before painting.

Anne Nicolle

Anne Nicolle's atelier.

Mehdi Mallier

Mehdi Mallier's atelier.

Bernard Pictet
p. 60: *Vulcain* gilded and chiselled glass.

Shaping a glass element in the atelier.

p. 64, above: Chiselled glass with a silver coating. Below: Reverse gilded glass. p. 65, above: Engraved glass with a leaf motif. Below: The chiselling process.

Steaven Richard

Steaven Richard's atelier.

Steaven with his fellow metalworkers and their tools.

Patrick Blanchard
The artist is pictured with floor lamps and two chests of drawers of his own design.

p. 76, above: Head of a cherub from an 18th-century altarpiece. Below and p. 77, above: Making an oak console table, a replica of one in the Musée des Arts Décoratifs, Paris. Below: Patrick's tools and working drawings.

Alain Bouchardon

Alain Bouchardon's atelier.

p. 82, above: Removal of varnish from a painting. Below: Canvas stretchers from various eras. p. 83, above: Removing the varnish from one section of a painting. Below: A few of the materials used during the restoration process.

Rémy Brazet

When re-covering an antique seat with its original tapestry, it is important to ensure that the upholstery retains its attractive curves throughout the process.

p. 88: Brocaded lampas and tasselled fringing used in the Empress's bedchamber at the Château de Fontainebleau.
p. 89: The atelier contains a huge collection of fabric samples from some of the world's greatest textile manufacturers.

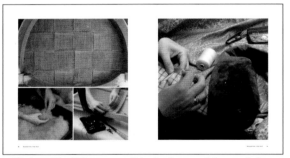

p. 90, above: The 18th-century webbing has been carefully reapplied to this chair and reinforced by adding an upper layer of new webbing. Below: Stuffing a chair seat. p. 91: Hand-stitching gives the piece a haute couture look and feel.

Details of a chair of gilded wood created by the furniture maker Bellangé for Madame Adélaïde, sister of King Louis-Philippe I of France. It is upholstered with ciselé velvet, finished with hand-stitched braid and piping cord.

Caroline Corrigan

Caroline Corrigan's atelier.

Youri Dmitrenko

p. 102: Preparing to restore a mirror frame from the Louis XV period.
p. 103: Gilded wood from the 17th, 18th and 19th centuries.

Marie Dubost

Marie Dubost's atelier.

Simon-Pierre Étienne

Simon-Pierre Étienne's atelier.

p. 114, left: Small table by Charles Topino.
p. 114, right, and p. 115, above: Details of a Louis XIV 'Mazarin' tiered bureau by Bernard van Risamburgh, in red tortoiseshell and brass marquetry.

Sébastien Evain

Sébastien Evain's atelier.

Gwénola Le Masson

Atelier L'Amarante, run by Gwénola Le Masson.

Rachida Mallogi

Rachida Mallogi's atelier.

Fernando Moreira
p. 134: Samples of exotic wood.

Matthieu Guillemot, specialist cabinetmaker. In the background, an array of cabinetmakers' tools can be seen.

p. 138, above: Arranging pieces of ebony and brass for a piece of Boulle marquetry. Below left: Gilded bronze handle from a chest of drawers by J. H. Riesner. Below right: A marquetry bouquet on a chest of drawers by J. H. Riesner. p. 139: Gilded bronze andiron with Triton, from a design by Antoine Moreau.

Aude Vieweger de Cordoüe & Thomas Vieweger

p. 142, above left: Plans for the restoration of the Grand Palais, Paris.
p. 143: Aude Vieweger de Cordoüe in her atelier.

Élise Blouet-Ménard

Élise Blouet-Ménard in her atelier.

p. 150: Leather is cut the old-fashioned way, with a knife, and linen thread is used for saddle-stitching. The atelier is full of tools and scraps of tanned leather that might be useful one day.
p. 151: A restored set of antique luggage in leather and metal.

Jacques Bolelli

Inside the Atelier Simon Marq.

Hervé Bruchet

Gérard Desquand

Gérard Desquand's atelier.

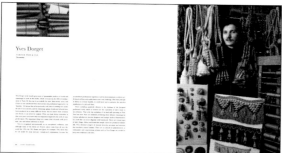

Yves Dorget

Yves Dorget's atelier.

Christian-Thierry Drevelle
p 170: Detail of an 18th-century gaming table, refurbished with a chequerboard design made up of samples of the many exotic woods used by the atelier.

The Atelier Drevelle is located in the town of Cognac in western France. It occupies a former wine storehouse designed by Gustave Eiffel.

p. 174, above right: A custom-made humidor in macassar wood. Below left: A wood veneer is applied. p. 175: This unusual seven-legged table, still under construction, is a reinterpretation of the Louis XV style. A similar piece was made for the Martell cognac house.

p. 176, above: Early sketches for the *Riva* case, designed for Veuve-Clicquot. p. 177: A humidor in figured mahogany, designed for a client who liked the idea of a humidor that resembled a travelling case.

Robert Jallet

Robert Jallet's atelier.

Patrick Fallon

A selection of leather cigar cases.

Reinhard von Nagel

Close-up view of the jacks inside a harpsichord. These pluck the strings to create the sound.

Details of some of the delicate work required when making a harpsichord.

Thomas Niemann

Thomas Niemann's atelier.

Laurent Nogues

Some designs from the Créanog atelier.

Nicolas Salagnac

Nicolas Salagnac's atelier.

p. 206, above: Engraving the steel matrix for the *Proserpina* medal (diameter 145 mm). Below: Engraver's hammers. p. 207, above: Steel matrices. Below: Preliminary plaster models for a bronze medallion (diameter 440 mm) based on a detail from Bernini's sculpture *The Rape of Proserpina*.

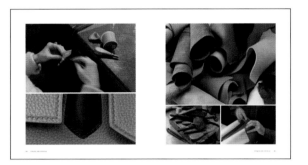

Serge Amoruso

Serge Amoruso's atelier.

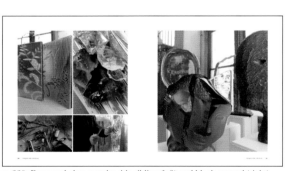

Gilles Chabrier

Gilles Chabrier chisels a glass sculpture in his atelier. On the left is the large glass head *Epigraph*, created in collaboration with Jacques Villeglé.

p. 220: Engraved glass panels with gilding (left) and black ground (right) applied on the reverse; blocks of uncut glass; tools for glass sculpting. p. 221: Deconstructed head in purple glass.

Pierre Corthay

Shoemaking tools.

p. 226, above: The cellar holds a library of shoe lasts. Below: Detail of the new Maison Corthay store. p. 227: Notebook and tools.

Sylvie Deschamps

The Bégonia d'Or atelier.

Caroline & Tristan Fournier

Caroline and Tristan Fournier's atelier.

Yves Gaignet
p. 238: Every ship's fittings are beautifully detailed and realistic.

p. 240, above, and p. 241: Yves works on a 1: 32 scale model of *Amazon*, a yacht designed by Sparkman & Stephens, built in 1971 by Camper & Nicholson. p. 240, below: Record book for the *Belem*, a model made for the Musée National de la Marine, Paris, containing notes and construction sketches, based on archive documents.

Dragui Romic & Arnaud Paix

At the Atelier Edgard Hamon, Arnaud Paix specializes in costume jewelry, while Dragui Romic concentrates on leatherwork.

Michel Heurtault

Michel Heurtault's atelier.

Françoise Hoffmann

Françoise Hoffmann's atelier.

p. 248, above: For an original piece of work based on a photograph, unspun wool is arranged over a layer of preprinted silk, then dampened. Below: When the wool is in position, the piece is covered with net, then soaped and fulled. p. 259: Some of Françoise's designs in the atelier.

Fanny Liautard

Fanny Liautard in her atelier.

p. 264, above: Sketching a design for a pleated dress.
p. 265: Details of a dress and coat in an Art Deco style, in tulle and Calais lace embroidered with glass beads.

Catherine Nicolas
p. 266: *Sea Dreams*, cuttlefish shells decorated with urushi lacquer, gold leaf and powdered gold.

Catherine Nicolas in her atelier. The panels will be lacquered and turned into a decorative mural.

p. 270, above: A bamboo tube called a *funzutsu* is used to scatter gold powder. Below left: A bowl of urushi lacquer and brushes; in the background are some ceramics in the *kintsugi* style: Below right: A bowl with decoration in eggshell inlay. p. 271: The trunk of a varnish tree (*Rhus vernicifera*), its bark cut with channels to gather the urushi lacquer.

Nelly Saunier

p. 274: Nelly in her atelier, surrounded by ostrich and turkey feathers.
p. 275, above: Dyed feathers from a silver pheasant. Below left: Jacquard design made of dyed and natural goose and pheasant feathers. Below right: Louboutin shoulder pieces, made of dyed goose, duck and rooster feathers.

Alain de Saint-Exupéry

Alain de Saint-Exupéry's atelier.

Jean-Luc Seigneur

Carving the design on a die used for embossing paper.

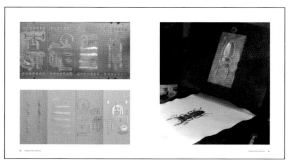

p. 284: Die (above) and embossed illustration (below) for the book *Le Couteau à grimaces (The Wincing Knife)*.
p. 285: Die and embossed illustration of a stag beetle.

Pietro Seminelli

Pietro Seminelli's atelier.

Christian Thirot

p. 294: Christian Thirot at a microscope in his atelier; a journal recording 33 years of sketches and projects; a range of supplies and tools.
p. 295: A selection of figurative ornaments in brass; adding handpainted lettering to the rings of a globe; a coat of arms in reversed gilded glass.

Fanny Boucher

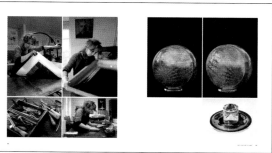

p. 300: Fanny Boucher in her atelier. p. 301: Works by Fanny Boucher. Above: *Protections*, engraved copper with ink and varnish inside a Plexiglas bubble. Below: *The Throne* by Roxane Rodriguez, heliographed copper disc (diameter 1.30 m), with Plexiglas element by Giovanni Scacchi.

Thierry Denis

Artisans at work in the ateliers.

Stéphane Guilbaud

Stéphane Guilbaud and his restored Voirin press.

Guillaume Martel & Manuela Paul-Cavallier

Manuela Paul-Cavallier and Guillaume Martel in their ateliers.

Étienne de Champfleury

Étienne de Champfleury's atelier.

Anne-Marie Msili-Jézéquel

p. 324: Anne-Marie colour-corrects an image on screen before printing.
p. 325: Preparing to make a print.

Didier Mutel

p. 328, above: *The Strange Case of Dr Jekyll and Mr Hyde*, artist's book, Robert Louis Stevenson and Didier Mutel, 1994. Below: *Manifeste de l'acide brut*, 2006. p. 329, left: Screenshots from the filmed performance *My Way*. Right: Tools and *No Acid, No Glory*, an engraving on walnut, 2012.

Jacky Vignon

Jacky Vignon's atelier.

Stéphane Bondu

Stéphane Bondu's atelier.

Christian Bonnet & Sons

p. 344: The measurements for each client are listed on a record sheet.
p. 345: Before adjusting the arm of a pair of spectacles, Franck heats it in the flame of a burner.

p. 346, above: The work of the Maison Bonnet on show at the Palais-Royal in Paris. Below: Tools and untreated tortoiseshell.
p. 347: The fixing of the hinges is done by hand, as is the polishing.

Anne-Lise Courchay

Anne-Lise Courchay's atelier.

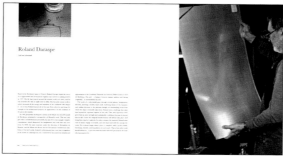

Roland Daraspe

p. 352: Sketchbooks filled with design ideas, a selection of tools, and a book with Coptic binding.
p. 353: A mosaic of kid parchment in a range of natural shades is arranged on a wood panel before being used to decorate an ebony cabinet.

p. 356, above: Roland Daraspe heats a goblet with a blowtorch. Below: *Aladdin* teapot; goblet with applied decoration; three-legged soup dish.
p. 357: Liqueur goblets and their designs; before engraving, a piece of silver is fixed in embossing cement; design for a soup dish; champagne goblets.

Frédéric Hamel

Fréderic Hamel's atelier.

Nicolas Marischael

Nicolas Marischael's atelier.

p. 368, above left: *Urban* teapot in solid silver, glass and ebony. Above right: Detail of a *Titan* candlestick in silver, glass and shagreen. Below: Restoration work in progress. p. 369: Samovar, teapot and sugar bowl in solid silver and algarrobo (an exotic wood).

Francis & Benoît Migeon

Francis Migeon's atelier.

Ludwig Vogelgesang
p. 374: Detail of a shagreen jewelry case.

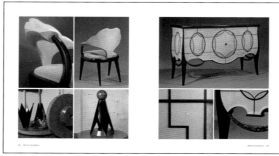

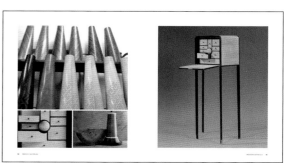

Ludwig Vogelgesang's atelier.

p. 378, above: Details of a *Ray* chair, in rosewood and shagreen. Below: Restoration of a pedestal table in amboyna wood and African ebony.
p. 379, above and below right: *Com Turri* sideboard in shagreen and carved ebony. Below left: Detail of a screen with shagreen decoration.

p. 380, above and below right: Lamp bases.
Below left and p. 381: Jewelry case in ebony and green-tinted shagreen.

Translated from the French *Les Grands Ateliers de France, vingt ans de métiers d'art* by David H. Wilson

First published in the United Kingdom in 2013 by
Thames & Hudson Ltd, 181A High Holborn, London WC1V 7QX

www.thamesandhudson.com

First published in 2013 in hardcover in the United States of America
by Thames & Hudson Inc., 500 Fifth Avenue, New York, New York 10110

thamesandhudsonusa.com

Original edition © 2013 Éditions Gourcuff-Gradenigo, Montreuil
This edition © 2013 Thames & Hudson Ltd, London

British Library Cataloguing-in-Publication Data
A catalogue record for this book is available from the British Library

Library of Congress Catalog Card Number 2013934845

ISBN: 978-0-500-51715-4

Printed and bound in France